JOYFUL
Lace

BY KNIT PICKS

Photography by Amy Cave

Printed in the United States of America

Second Printing, 2016

ISBN 9781627671255

Versa Press, Inc
800-447-7829

www.versapress.com

CONTENTS

SHIFTING LACE SHAWL

by Clare Lakewood

FINISHED MEASUREMENTS

27 (43)" back depth, 54 (86)" wide at widest point

YARN

Knit Picks Palette (100% Peruvian Highland Wool; 231 yards/50g): Comfrey 26050, 2 (4) balls.

NEEDLES

US 7 (4.5mm) 24" or longer circular needles, or size to obtain gauge

NOTIONS

4 Stitch Markers
Yarn Needle

GAUGE

14 sts and 26 rows = 4" over Lace Pattern 1, blocked.

Shifting Lace Shawl

Notes:

This shawl may be customized by repeating Lace Patterns 1 and 2 as many or as few times as desired. To repeat Lace Pattern 1, after working Rows 1-28, repeat Rows 13-28 as many times as desired. To repeat Lace Pattern 2, work rows 1-48 as many times as desired, then work rows 1-42. Adding additional repeats, will, of course, increase the quantity of yarn needed to complete the shawl.

Charts show RS rows only, and are worked from the bottom up, and followed from right to left. WS rows are not shown in the charts. For each WS row, K2, SM, P to M, SM, P1, SM, P to M, SM, K2, creating a Garter st edging. Do not work a WS row after Row 23 of Lace Pattern 3.

Lace Pattern 1 (worked flat)

Row 1 (RS): SL 1, K1, SM, YO, K1, YO, SM, K1, SM, YO, K1, YO, SM, K2. (4 sts inc.)

Row 2 and all WS Rows through Row 28: SL 1, K1, SM, P to M, SM, P1, SM, P to M, SM, K2.

Row 3: SL 1, K1, SM, YO, K3, YO, SM, K1, SM, YO, K3, YO, SM, K2. (4 sts inc.)

Row 5: SL 1, K1, SM, YO, K5, YO, SM, K1, SM, YO, K5, YO, SM, K2. (4 sts inc.)

Row 7: SL 1, K1, SM, YO, K1, YO, SSK, K1, K2TOG, YO, K1, YO, SM, K1, SM, YO, K1, YO, SSK, K1, K2TOG, YO, K1, YO, SM, K2. (4 sts inc.)

Row 9: SL 1, K1, SM, YO, K1, SSK, (K1, YO) twice, K1, K2TOG, K1, YO, SM, K1, SM, YO, K1, SSK, (K1, YO) twice, K1, K2TOG, K1, YO, SM, K2. (4 sts inc.)

Row 11: SL, K1, SM, YO, K2, SSK, YO, K3, YO, K2TOG, K2, YO, SM, K1, SM, YO, K2, SSK, YO, K3, YO, K2TOG, K2, YO, SM, K2. (4 sts inc.)

Row 13: SL 1, K1, SM, YO, K2TOG, YO, K1, (YO, K1, SSK, K1, K2TOG, K1, YO, K1) to 2 sts before M, YO, SSK, YO, SM, K1, SM, YO, K2TOG, YO, K1, (YO, K1, SSK, K1, K2TOG, K1, YO, K1) to last 2 sts, YO, SSK, YO, SM, K2. (4 sts inc.)

Row 15: SL 1, K1, SM, YO, K2TOG, YO, K2, (K1, YO, SSK, K1, K2TOG, YO, K2) to 3 sts before M, K1, YO, SSK, YO, SM, K1, SM, YO, K2TOG, YO, K2, (K1, YO, SSK, K1, K2TOG, YO, K2) to 3 sts before M, K1, YO, SSK, YO, SM, K2. (4 sts inc.)

Row 17: SL 1, K1, SM, (YO, K1) twice, K2TOG, K1, (SSK, (K1, YO) twice, K1, K2TOG, K1) to 4 sts before M, SSK, (K1, YO) twice, SM, K1, SM, (YO, K1) twice, K2TOG, K1, (SSK, (K1, YO) twice, K1, K2TOG, K1) to 4 sts before M, SSK, (K1, YO) twice, SM, K2. (4 sts inc.)

Row 19: SL 1, K1, SM, YO, K3, YO, K2TOG, K1, (SSK, YO, K3, YO, K2TOG, K1) to 5 sts before M, SSK, YO, K3, YO, SM, K1, SM, YO, K3, YO, K2TOG, K1, (SSK, YO, K3, YO, K2TOG, K1) to 5 sts before M, SSK, YO, K3, YO, SM, K2. (4 sts inc.)

Row 21: SL 1, K1, SM, YO, K3, K2TOG, K1, YO, K1, (YO, K1, SSK, K1, K2TOG, K1, YO, K1) to 6 sts before M, YO, K1, SSK, K3, YO, SM, K1, SM, YO, K3, K2TOG, K1, YO, K1, (YO, K1, SSK, K1, K2TOG, K1, YO, K1) to 6 sts before M, YO, K1, SSK, K3, YO, SM, K2. (4 sts inc.)

Row 23: SL 1, K1, SM, YO, K1, YO, SSK, K1, K2TOG, YO, K2, (K1 YO, SSK, K1, K2TOG, YO, K2) to 7 sts before M, K1, YO, SSK, K1, K2TOG, YO, K1, YO, SM, K1, SM, YO, K1, YO, SSK, K1, K2TOG, YO, K2, (K1 YO, SSK, K1, K2TOG, YO, K2) to 7 sts before M, K1, YO, SSK, K1, K2TOG,

YO, K1, YO, SM, K2. (4 sts inc.)

Row 25: SL 1, K1, SM, YO, K1, SSK, (K1 YO) twice, K1, K2TOG, K1, (SSK, (K1 YO) twice, K1, K2TOG, K1) to 8 sts before M, SSK, (K1 YO) twice, K1, K2TOG, K1, YO, SM, K1, SM, YO, K1, SSK, (K1 YO) twice, K1, K2TOG, K1, (SSK, (K1 YO) twice, K1, K2TOG, K1) to 8 sts before M, SSK, (K1 YO) twice, K1, K2TOG, K1, YO, SM, K2. (4 sts inc.)

Row 27: SL 1, K1, SM, YO, K2, SSK, YO, K3, YO, K2TOG, K1, (SSK, YO, K3, YO, K2TOG, K1) to 9 sts before M, SSK, YO, K3, YO, K2TOG, K2, YO, SM, K1, SM, YO, K2, SSK, YO, K3, YO, K2TOG, K1, (SSK, YO, K3, YO, K2TOG, K1) to 9 sts before M, SSK, YO, K3, YO, K2TOG, K2, YO, SM, K2. (4 sts inc.)

Lace Pattern 2 (worked flat)

Row 1 (RS): SL 1, K1, SM, YO, K3, (K2TOG, YO, K3, YO, SSK, K1) until 2 sts from M, K2, YO, SM, K1, SM, YO, K3, (K2TOG, YO, K3, YO, SSK, K1) until 2 sts from M, K2, YO, SM, K2. (4 sts inc.)

Row 2 and all WS Rows through Row 48: SL 1, K1, SM, P to M, SM, P1, SM, P to M, SM, K2.

Row 3: SL 1, K1, SM, YO, K2, YO, SK2P, (YO, K5, YO, SK2P) until 2 sts from M, YO, K2, YO, SM, K1, SM, YO, K2, YO, SK2P, (YO, K5, YO, SK2P) until 2 sts from M, YO, K2, YO, SM, K2. (4 sts inc.)

Row 5: SL 1, K1, SM, YO, K1, K2TOG, K1, YO, K1, (YO, K1, SSK, K1, K2TOG, K1, YO, K1) until 4 sts from M, YO, K1, SSK, K1, YO, SM, K1, SM, YO, K1, K2TOG, K1, YO, K1, (YO, K1, SSK, K1, K2TOG, K1, YO, K1) until 4 sts from M, YO, K1, SSK, K1, YO, SM, K2. (4 sts inc.)

Row 7: SL 1, K1, SM, YO, K2, K2TOG, K1, YO, K1, (YO, K1, SSK, K1, K2TOG, K1, YO, K1) until 5 sts from M, YO, K1, SSK, K2, YO, SM, K1, SM, YO, K2, K2TOG, K1, YO, K1, (YO, K1, SSK, K1, K2TOG, K1, YO, K1) until 5 sts from M, YO, K1, SSK, K2, YO, SM, K2. (4 sts inc.)

Row 9: SL 1, K1, SM, YO, K2TOG, YO, K1, YO, SSK, K2, (K1, K2TOG, YO, K1, YO, SSK, K2) until 6 sts from M, K1, K2TOG, YO, K1, YO, SSK, YO, SM, K1, SM, YO, K2TOG, YO, K1, YO, SSK, K2, (K1, K2TOG, YO, K1, YO, SSK, K2) until 6 sts from M, K1, K2TOG, YO, K1, YO, SSK, YO, SM, K2. (4 sts inc.)

Row 11: SL 1, K1, SM, YO, K2TOG, YO, K3, YO, SSK, K1, (K2TOG, YO, K3, YO, SSK, K1) until 7 sts from M, K2TOG, YO, K3, YO, SSK, YO, SM, K1, SM, YO, K2TOG, YO, K3, YO, SSK, K1, (K2TOG, YO, K3, YO, SSK, K1) until 7 sts from M, K2TOG, YO, K3, YO, SSK, YO, SM, K2. (4 sts inc.)

Row 13: SL 1, K1, SM, (YO, K2TOG) twice, YO, K1, YO, SSK, YO, SK2P, (YO, K2TOG, YO, K1, YO, SSK, YO, SK2P) until 7 sts from M, YO, K2TOG, YO, K1, (YO, SSK) twice, YO, SM, K1, SM, (YO, K2TOG) twice, YO, K1, YO, SSK, YO, SK2P, (YO, K2TOG, YO, K1, YO, SSK, YO, SK2P) until 7 sts from M, YO, K2TOG, YO, K1, (YO, SSK) twice, YO, SM, K2. (4 sts inc.)

Row 15: SL 1, K1, SM, YO, K2, K2TOG, YO, K3, YO, SSK, K1, (K2TOG, YO, K3, YO, SSK, K1) until 9 sts from M, K2TOG, YO, K3, YO, SSK, K2, YO, SM, K1, SM, YO, K2, K2TOG, YO, K3, YO, SSK, K1, (K2TOG, YO, K3, YO, SSK, K1) until 9 sts from M, K2TOG, YO, K3, YO, SSK, K2, YO, SM, K2. (4 sts inc.)

Row 17: SL 1, K1, SM, YO, K1, YO, SK2P, YO, K5, YO, SK2P, (YO, K5, YO, SK2P) until 9 sts from M, YO, K5, YO, SK2P, YO, K1, YO, SM, K1, SM, YO, K1, YO, SK2P, YO, K5, YO, SK2P, (YO, K5, YO, SK2P) until 9 sts from M, YO, K5, YO, SK2P, YO, K1, YO, SM, K2. (4 sts inc.)

Row 19: SL 1, K1, SM, YO, K5, K2TOG, YO, K1, YO, SSK, K2, (K1, K2TOG, YO, K1, YO, SSK, K2) until 11 sts from M, K1, K2TOG, YO, K1,

YO, SSK, K5, YO, SM, K1, SM, YO, K5, K2TOG, YO, K1, YO, SSK, K2, (K1, K2TOG, YO, K1, YO, SSK, K2) until 11 sts from M, K1, K2TOG, YO, K1, YO, SSK, K5, YO, SM, K2. (4 sts inc.)

Row 21: SL 1, K1, SM, YO, K2, YO, SSK, K1, K2TOG, YO, K3, YO, SSK, K1, (K2TOG, YO, K3, YO, SSK, K1) until 12 sts from M, K2TOG, YO, K3, YO, SSK, K1, K2TOG, YO, K2, YO, SM, K1, SM, YO, K2, YO, SSK, K1, K2TOG, YO, K3, YO, SSK, K1, (K2TOG, YO, K3, YO, SSK, K1) until 12 sts from M, K2TOG, YO, K3, YO, SSK, K1, K2TOG, YO, K2, YO, SM, K2. (4 sts inc.)

Row 23: SL 1, K1, SM, YO, K2, YO, SSK, YO, SK2P, YO, K2TOG, YO, K1, YO, SSK, YO, SK2P, (YO, K2TOG, YO, K1, YO, SSK, YO, SK2P) until 12 sts from M, YO, K2TOG, YO, K1, YO, SSK, YO, SK2P, YO, K2TOG, YO, K2, YO, SM, K1, SM, YO, K2, YO, SSK, YO, SK2P, YO, K2TOG, YO, K1, YO, SSK, YO, SK2P, (YO, K2TOG, YO, K1, YO, SSK, YO, SK2P) until 12 sts from M, YO, K2TOG, YO, K1, YO, SSK, YO, SK2P, YO, K2TOG, YO, K2, YO, SM, K2. (4 sts inc.)

Row 25: SL 1, K1, SM, YO, K4, YO, SSK, K1, K2TOG, YO, K3, YO, SSK, K1, (K2TOG, YO, K3, YO, SSK, K1) until 14 sts from M, K2TOG, YO, K3, YO, SSK, K1, K2TOG, YO, K4, YO, SM, K1, SM, YO, K4, YO, SSK, K1, K2TOG, YO, K3, YO, SSK, K1, (K2TOG, YO, K3, YO, SSK, K1) until 14 sts from M, K2TOG, YO, K3, YO, SSK, K1, K2TOG, YO, K4, YO, SM, K2. (4 sts inc.)

Row 27: SL 1, K1, SM, YO, K6, YO, SK2P, YO, K5, YO, SK2P, (YO, K5, YO, SK2P) until 14 sts from M, YO, K5, YO, SK2P, YO, K6, YO, SM, K1, SM, YO, K6, YO, SK2P, YO, K5, YO, SK2P, (YO, K5, YO, SK2P) until 14 sts from M, YO, K5, YO, SK2P, YO, K6, YO, SM, K2. (4 sts inc.)

Row 29: SL 1, K1, SM, *(YO, K1) twice, SSK, K1, K2TOG, K1; rep from * once more, YO, K1, (YO, K1, SSK, K1, K2TOG, K1, YO, K1) until 16 sts from M, (YO, K1, SSK, K1, K2TOG, K1, YO, K1) twice, YO, SM, K1, SM, *(YO, K1) twice, SSK, K1, K2TOG, K1; rep from * once more, YO, K1, (YO, K1, SSK, K1, K2TOG, K1, YO, K1) until 16 sts from M, (YO, K1, SSK, K1, K2TOG, K1, YO, K1) twice, YO, SM, K2. (4 sts inc.)

Row 31: SL 1, K1, SM, YO, K2, (YO, K1, SSK, K1, K2TOG, K1, YO, K1) twice, (YO, K1, SSK, K1, K2TOG, K1, YO, K1) until 17 sts from M, YO, K1, SSK, K1, K2TOG, (K1, YO) twice, K1, SSK, K1, K2TOG, K1, YO, K2, YO, SM, K1, SM, YO, K2, (YO, K1, SSK, K1, K2TOG, K1, YO, K1) twice, (YO, K1, SSK, K1, K2TOG, K1, YO, K1) until 17 sts from M, YO, K1, SSK, K1, K2TOG, (K1, YO) twice, K1, SSK, K1, K2TOG, K1, YO, K2, YO, SM, K2. (4 sts inc.)

Row 33: SL 1, K1, SM, YO, K4, K2TOG, YO, K1, YO, SSK, K3, K2TOG, YO, K1, YO, SSK, K2, (K1, K2TOG, YO, K1, YO, SSK, K2) until 18 sts from M, K1, K2TOG, YO, K1, YO, SSK, K3, K2TOG, YO, K1, YO, SSK, K4, YO, SM, K1, SM, YO, K4, K2TOG, YO, K1, YO, SSK, K3, K2TOG, YO, K1, YO, SSK, K2, (K1, K2TOG, YO, K1, YO, SSK, K2) until 18 sts from M, K1, K2TOG, YO, K1, YO, SSK, K3, K2TOG, YO, K1, YO, SSK, K4, YO, SM, K2. (4 sts inc.)

Row 35: SL 1, K1, SM, YO, K1, (YO, SSK, K1, K2TOG, YO, K3) twice, YO, SSK, K1, (K2TOG, YO, K3, YO, SSK, K1) until 19 sts from M, (K2TOG, YO, K3, YO, SSK, K1) twice, K2TOG, YO, K1, YO, SM, K1, SM, YO, K1, (YO, SSK, K1, K2TOG, YO, K3) twice, YO, SSK, K1, (K2TOG, YO, K3, YO, SSK, K1) until 19 sts from M, (K2TOG, YO, K3, YO, SSK, K1) twice, K2TOG, YO, K1, YO, SM, K2. (4 sts inc.)

Row 37: SL 1, K1, SM, (YO, K1, YO, SSK, YO, SK2P, YO, K2TOG) twice, YO, K1, YO, SSK, YO, SK2P, (YO, K2TOG, YO, K1, YO, SSK, YO, SK2P) until 19 sts from M, (YO, K2TOG, YO, K1, YO, SSK, YO, SK2P) twice, YO, K2TOG, YO, K1, YO, SM, K1, SM, (YO, K1, YO, SSK,

YO, SK2P, YO, K2TOG) twice, YO, K1, YO, SSK, YO, SK2P, (YO, K2TOG, YO, K1, YO, SSK, YO, SK2P) until 19 sts from M, (YO, K2TOG, YO, K1, YO, SSK, YO, SK2P) twice, YO, K2TOG, YO, K1, YO, SM, K2. (4 sts inc.)

Row 39: SL 1, K1, SM, (YO, K3, YO, SSK, K1, K2TOG) twice, YO, K3, YO, SSK, K1, (K2TOG, YO, K3, YO, SSK, K1) until 21 sts from M, (K2TOG, YO, K3, YO, SSK, K1) twice, K2TOG, YO, K3, YO, SM, K1, SM, (YO, K3, YO, SSK, K1, K2TOG) twice, YO, K3, YO, SSK, K1, (K2TOG, YO, K3, YO, SSK, K1) until 21 sts from M, (K2TOG, YO, K3, YO, SSK, K1) twice, K2TOG, YO, K3, YO, SM, K2. (4 sts inc.)

Row 41: SL 1, K1, SM, (YO, K5, YO, SK2P) 3 times, (YO, K5, YO, SK2P) until 21 sts from M, (YO, K5, YO, SK2P) twice, YO, K5, YO, SM, K1, SM, (YO, K5, YO, SK2P) 3 times, (YO, K5, YO, SK2P) until 21 sts from M, (YO, K5, YO, SK2P) twice, YO, K5, YO, SM, K2. (4 sts inc.)

Row 43: SL 1, K1, SM, YO, K1, (K2TOG, YO, K1, YO, SSK, K3) twice, K2TOG, YO, K1, YO, SSK, K2, (K1, K2TOG, YO, K1, YO, SSK, K2) until 23 sts from M, K1, (K2TOG, YO, K1, YO, SSK, K3) twice, K2TOG, YO, K1, YO, SSK, K1, YO, SM, K1, SM, YO, K1, (K2TOG, YO, K1, YO, SSK, K3) twice, K2TOG, YO, K1, YO, SSK, K2, (K1, K2TOG, YO, K1, YO, SSK, K2) until 23 sts from M, K1, (K2TOG, YO, K1, YO, SSK, K3) twice, K2TOG, YO, K1, YO, SSK, K1, YO, SM, K2. (4 sts inc.)

Row 45: SL 1, K1, SM, YO, (K1, K2TOG, YO, K3, YO, SSK) 3 times, K1, (K2TOG, YO, K3, YO, SSK, K1) until 24 sts from M, (K2TOG, YO, K3, YO, SSK, K1) 3 times, YO, SM, K1, SM, YO, (K1, K2TOG, YO, K3, YO, SSK) 3 times, K1, (K2TOG, YO, K3, YO, SSK, K1) until 24 sts from M, (K2TOG, YO, K3, YO, SSK, K1) 3 times, YO, SM, K2. (4 sts inc.)

Row 47: SL 1, K1, SM, YO, K1, K2TOG, (YO, K2TOG, YO, K1, YO, SSK, YO, SK2P) 3 times, (YO, K2TOG, YO, K1, YO, SSK, YO, SK2P) until 24 sts from M, (YO, K2TOG, YO, K1, YO, SSK, YO, SK2P) twice, YO, K2TOG, YO, K1, (YO, SSK) twice, K1, YO, SM, K1, SM, YO, K1, K2TOG, (YO, K2TOG, YO, K1, YO, SSK, YO, SK2P) 3 times, (YO, K2TOG, YO, K1, YO, SSK, YO, SK2P) until 24 sts from M, (YO, K2TOG, YO, K1, YO, SSK, YO, SK2P) twice, YO, K2TOG, YO, K1, (YO, SSK) twice, K1, YO, SM, K2. (4 sts inc.)

Lace Pattern 3 (worked flat)

Row 1 (RS): SL 1, K1, SM, YO, K4, (K3, YO, SSK, K5, K2TOG, YO, K4) until 3 sts from M, K3, YO, SM, K1, SM, YO, K4, (K3, YO, SSK, K5, K2TOG, YO, K4) until 3 sts from M, K3, YO, SM, K2. (4 sts inc.)

Row 2 and all WS Rows through Row 22: SL 1, K1, SM, P to M, SM, P1, SM, P to M, SM, K2.

Row 3: SL 1, K1, SM, (YO, K1) twice, SSK, K1, (K2TOG, (K1, YO) twice, SSK, K3, K2TOG, (YO, K1) twice, SSK, K1) until 4 sts from M, K2TOG, (K1, YO) twice, SM, K1, SM, (YO, K1) twice, SSK, K1, (K2TOG, (K1, YO) twice, SSK, K3, K2TOG, (YO, K1) twice, SSK, K1) until 4 sts from M, K2TOG, (K1, YO) twice, SM, K2. (4 sts inc.)

Row 5: SL 1, K1, SM, YO, K3, YO, SSK, K1, (K2TOG, YO, K3, YO, SSK, K1) until 5 sts from M, K2TOG, YO, K3, YO, SM, K1, SM, YO, K3, YO, SSK, K1, (K2TOG, YO, K3, YO, SSK, K1) until 5 sts from M, K2TOG, YO, K3, YO, SM, K2. (4 sts inc.)

Row 7: SL 1, K1, SM, YO, K3, SSK, K1, YO, K1, (YO, K1, K2TOG, K3, YO, SK2P, YO, K3, SSK, K1, YO, K1) until 6 sts from M, YO, K1, K2TOG, K3, YO, SM, K1, SM, YO, K3, SSK, K1, YO, K1, (YO, K1, K2TOG, K3, YO, SK2P, YO, K3, SSK, K1, YO, K1) until 6 sts from M, YO, K1, K2TOG, K3, YO, SM, K2. (4 sts inc.)

Row 9: SL 1, K1, SM, YO, K4, SSK, YO, K2, (K1, YO, K2TOG, K3, YO,

SK2P, YO, K3, SSK, YO, K2) until 7 sts from M, K1, YO, K2TOG, K4, YO, SM, K1, SM, YO, K4, SSK, YO, K2, (K1, YO, K2TOG, K3, YO, SK2P, YO, K3, SSK, YO, K2) until 7 sts from M, K1, YO, K2TOG, K4, YO, SM, K2. (4 sts inc.)

Row 11: SL 1, K1, SM, YO, K1, YO, SSK, K2, SSK, YO, K2, (K1, YO, K2TOG, K3, YO, SK2P, YO, K3, SSK, YO, K2) until 8 sts from M, K1, YO, K2TOG, K2, K2TOG, YO, K1, YO, SM, K1, SM, YO, K1, YO, SSK, K2, SSK, YO, K2, (K1, YO, K2TOG, K3, YO, SK2P, YO, K3, SSK, YO, K2) until 8 sts from M, K1, YO, K2TOG, K2, K2TOG, YO, K1, YO, SM, K2. (4 sts inc.)

Row 13: SL 1, K1, SM, YO, K3, YO, SSK, K3, YO, SK2P, (YO, K3, K2TOG, YO, K3, YO, SSK, K3, YO, SK2P) until 8 sts from M, YO, K3, K2TOG, YO, K3, YO, SM, K1, SM, YO, K3, YO, SSK, K3, YO, SK2P, (YO, K3, K2TOG, YO, K3, YO, SSK, K3, YO, SK2P) until 8 sts from M, YO, K3, K2TOG, YO, K3, YO, SM, K2. (4 sts inc.)

Row 15: SL 1, K1, SM, YO, K5, YO, SSK, K2TOG, YO, K2, (K1, YO, SSK, K2TOG, YO, K5, YO, SSK, K2TOG, YO, K2) until 10 sts from M, K1, YO, SSK, K2TOG, YO, K5, YO, SM, K1, SM, YO, K5, YO, SSK, K2TOG, YO, K2, (K1, YO, SSK, K2TOG, YO, K5, YO, SSK, K2TOG, YO, K2) until 10 sts from M, K1, YO, SSK, K2TOG, YO, K5, YO, SM, K2. (4 sts inc.)

Row 17: SL 1, K1, SM, YO, K7, YO, SSK, YO, K2TOG, K1, (SSK, YO, K2TOG, YO, K7, YO, SSK, YO, K2TOG, K1) until 11 sts from M, SSK, YO, K2TOG, YO, K7, YO, SM, K1, SM, YO, K7, YO, SSK, YO, K2TOG, K1, (SSK, YO, K2TOG, YO, K7, YO, SSK, YO, K2TOG, K1) until 11 sts from M, SSK, YO, K2TOG, YO, K7, YO, SM, K2. (4 sts inc.)

Row 19: SI, K1, SM, YO, K1, YO, K2, SK2P, K2, YO, K1, YO, SSK, K2, (K1, K2TOG, YO, K1, YO, K2, SK2P, K2, YO, K1, YO, SSK, K2) until 12 sts from M, K1, K2TOG, YO, K1, YO, K2, SK2P, K2, YO, K1, YO, SM, K1, SM, YO, K1, YO, K2, SK2P, K2, YO, K1, YO, SSK, K2, (K1, K2TOG, YO, K1, YO, K2, SK2P, K2, YO, K1, YO, SSK, K2) until 12 sts from M, K1, K2TOG, YO, K1, YO, K2, SK2P, K2, YO, K1, YO, SM, K2. (4 sts inc.)

Row 21: SI, K1, SM, (YO, K1) twice, YO, SSK, SK2P, K2TOG, (YO, K1) twice, YO, SSK, K1, (K2TOG, (YO, K1) twice, YO, SSK, SK2P, K2TOG, (YO, K1) twice, YO, SSK, K1) until 13 sts from M, K2TOG, (YO, K1) twice, YO, SSK, SK2P, K2TOG, (YO, K1) twice, YO, SM, K1, SM, (YO, K1) twice, YO, SSK, SK2P, K2TOG, (YO, K1) twice, YO, SSK, K1, (K2TOG, (YO, K1) twice, YO, SSK, SK2P, K2TOG, (YO, K1) twice, YO, SSK, K1) until 13 sts from M, K2TOG, (YO, K1) twice, YO, SSK, SK2P, K2TOG, (YO, K1) twice, YO, SM, K2. (4 sts inc.)

Row 23: SI, K1, SM, (YO, K2TOG) twice, YO, K1, YO, SK2P, YO, K1, (YO, SSK) twice, YO, SK2P, ((YO, K2TOG) twice, YO, K1, YO, SK2P, YO, K1, (YO, SSK) twice, YO, SK2P) until 13 sts from M, (YO, K2TOG) twice, YO, K1, YO, SK2P, YO, K1, (YO, SSK) twice, YO, SM, K1, SM, (YO, K2TOG) twice, YO, K1, YO, SK2P, YO, K1, (YO, SSK) twice, YO, SK2P, ((YO, K2TOG) twice, YO, K1, YO, SK2P, YO, K1, (YO, SSK) twice, YO, SK2P) until 13 sts from M, (YO, K2TOG) twice, YO, K1, YO, SK2P, YO, K1, (YO, SSK) twice, YO, SM, K2. (4 sts inc.)

Elastic Lace Bind Off

Lace needs an especially elastic bind off, so that the bound off edge can be stretched into the desired border shape. The following is suitable: P2, *SI 2 sts just worked back onto left-hand needles, P2TOG, P1; repeat from * as many times as necessary. When 1 st remains, cut yarn and thread through st. Pull tight.

DIRECTIONS

Garter Tab Cast On

CO 2 sts. K 6 rows. Keeping 2 live sts on left needle, PU and K 3 sts along long side of garter tab, then PU and K 2 sts from CO edge. (7 sts total)

SI 2, PM, SI 1, PM, SI 1, PM, SI 1, PM. Move all sts on right needle back to left needle.

Shawlette

Rows 1-28: Work Rows 1-28 of Lace Pattern 1. (63 sts)

Rows 29-44: Rep Rows 13 – 28 of Lace Pattern 1 once more. (95 sts)

Rows 45-86: Work Rows 1-42 of Lace Pattern 2. (179 sts)

Rows 87-109: Work Rows 1-23 of Lace Pattern 3. (227 sts)

Shawl

Rows 1-28: Work Rows 1-28 of Lace Pattern 1. (63 sts)

Rows 29-60: Rep Rows 13-28 of Lace Pattern 1 two more times. (127 sts)

Rows 61-108: Work Rows 1-48 of Lace Pattern 2. (223 sts)

Rows 109 to 150: Rep Rows 1-42 of Lace Pattern 2 once more. (307 sts)

Rows 151-173: Work Rows 1-23 of Lace Pattern 3. (355 sts)

Finishing

Bind off, using Elastic Lace Bind Off. Weave in ends, wash and block to diagram.

Lace Pattern 1

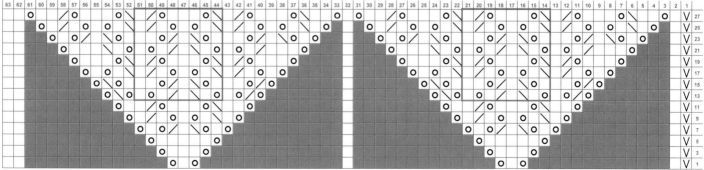

Legend

slip
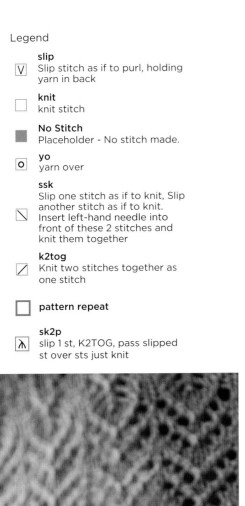
Slip stitch as if to purl, holding yarn in back

knit
knit stitch

No Stitch
Placeholder - No stitch made.

yo
yarn over

ssk
Slip one stitch as if to knit, Slip another stitch as if to knit. Insert left-hand needle into front of these 2 stitches and knit them together

k2tog
Knit two stitches together as one stitch

pattern repeat

sk2p
slip 1 st, K2TOG, pass slipped st over sts just knit

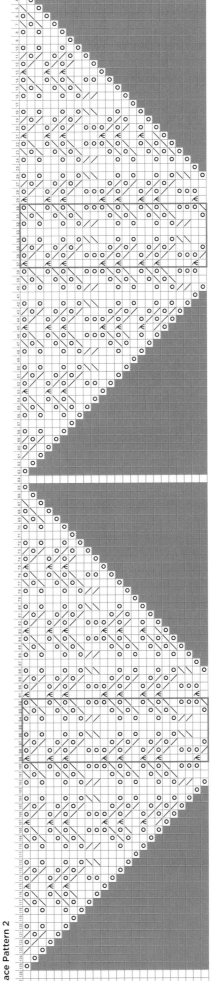

Lace Pattern 2

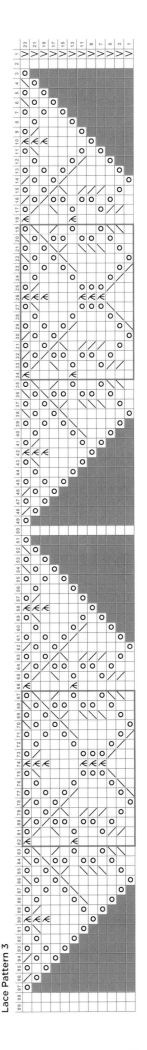

Lace Pattern 3

PHAROS SHAWL

by Joyce Fassbender

FINISHED MEASUREMENTS
52" x 52" square, blocked.

YARN
Knit Picks Alpaca Cloud Lace (100% Baby Alpaca; 440 yards/50g): Willoughby 26806, 4 skeins.

NEEDLES
US size 3 (3.25mm) DPNs, 24" and 36" long circular needles, or size to obtain gauge

NOTIONS
Yarn Needle
Stitch Markers
Cable Needle

GAUGE
24 sts and 28 rows = 4" in St st, blocked.

Pharos Shawl

Notes:

This is a square shawl that is knit from the center to the outer edges. Yarn over increases at each end of the chart are used to form the square shape. Increases are worked on odd numbered rows only for charts A – E, but are worked on odd and even rows on chart F. Odd and even rows are worked from right to left. For charts, work each odd row as follows: * work chart* four times. Even rows are included on the charts and should be worked as follows: * work chart* four times.

Boxed areas of charts represent stitch pattern repeat across rows. Use stitch markers between panels and stitch pattern repeats if necessary. Stitch markers between stitch pattern repeats will need to be repositioned between charts, including between repeats of Chart B. Please see instructions below for additional information.

In order to increase the size of the shawl, work additional repeats of chart B. Each added repeat will result in an increase of 128 stitches per row.

Circular Cast On

Pinch the working yarn between the first and middle finger of your left hand so the end of the yarn comes out behind your fingers. Wrap the working yarn tail around the ring and pinky fingers of your left hand, holding the yarn tail firmly with your right hand. Point the tips of these fingers down toward your palm. *Using your right hand, insert the point of your needle (you can use DPNs or a circular) under the yarn across the back of your ring and pinky fingers (the 'first loop') from front to back. Pass the needle over the working yarn and draw a loop out from under the first loop; this creates one cast-on st. YO.* Repeat from * to * until you have cast on the required number of sts. Note: If you need an even number of sts, you will need to cast on the final st as a standard yarn over when you begin your first round of knitting. Arrange the sts on your DPNs to begin knitting in the round.

Tug on the yarn tail to draw the sts into a tighter circle.

C4B (cable four back): Sl 2 sts to CN and hold in back. K2, K2 sts from CN.

C4F (cable four front): Sl 2 sts to CN and hold in front. K2, K2 sts from CN.

K2tog Bind Off: K2, sl sts onto left needle, K2tog TBL, *K1, sl sts onto left needle, K2tog TBL*, repeat from * to * until all sts are bound off.

DIRECTIONS

CO 4 sts using Circular Cast On. PM and join in the round taking care not to twist sts. K all sts. Switch to progressively longer circular needles as needed when working the charts.

Work Rows 1-16 of Chart A one time. 68 sts.
Work Rows 1-32 of Chart B four times. Work boxed stitch pattern one time for the first repeat, three times for the second repeat, five times for the third repeat, and seven times for the fourth repeat. 580 sts.

Work Rows 1-16 of Chart C one time. Work boxed stitch pattern repeat eight times. 644 sts.

Work Rows 1-16 of Chart D one time. Work boxed stitch pattern repeat four times. 708 sts.

Work Rows 1-22 of Chart E one time. Work boxed stitch pattern repeat five times. 788 sts.

Work Rows 1-17 of Chart F one time. Work boxed stitch pattern repeat six times. 924 sts.

Finishing

BO very loosely using K2tog Bind Off. Weave in ends and block to diagram.

Legend

■	**No Stitch**	Placeholder - No stitch made.
▢O	**yo**	Yarn Over
▢	**knit**	knit stitch
▢•	**purl**	purl stitch
╱	**k2tog**	Knit two stitches together as one stitch
╲	**ssk**	Slip one stitch as if to knit, Slip another stitch as if to knit. Insert left-hand needle into front of these 2 stitches and knit them together
▢	**pattern repeat**	
⋏	**sl1 k2tog psso**	slip 1, k2tog, pass slip stitch over k2tog
⫻	**k3tog**	Knit three stitches together as one
⊠	**cable 4 back (c4b)**	sl2 to CN, hold in back. k2, k2 from CN
⊠	**cable 4 front (c4f)**	sl 2 to CN, hold in front. k2, k2 from CN
⋀	**s2, k1, p2sso**	Slip first and second stitches together as if to knit. Knit 1 stitch. Pass two slipped stitches over the knit stitch.

Chart A

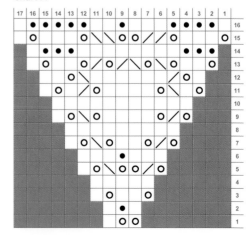

Chart B

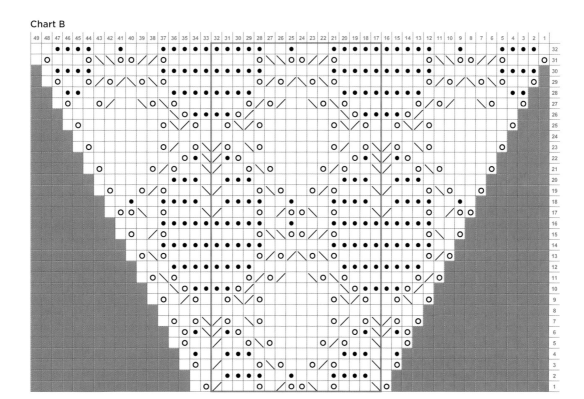

Chart C

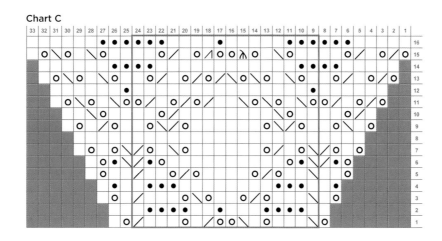

Chart D

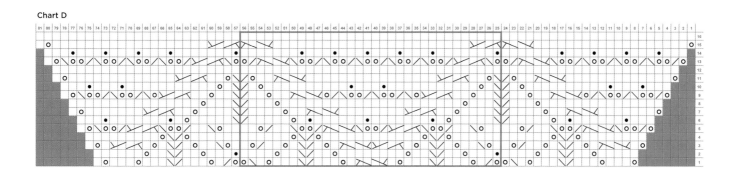

Chart E

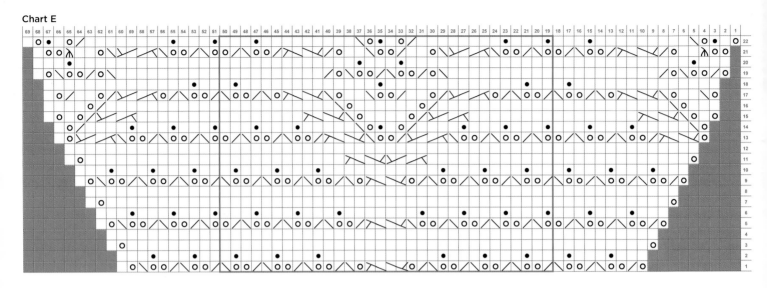

Chart F

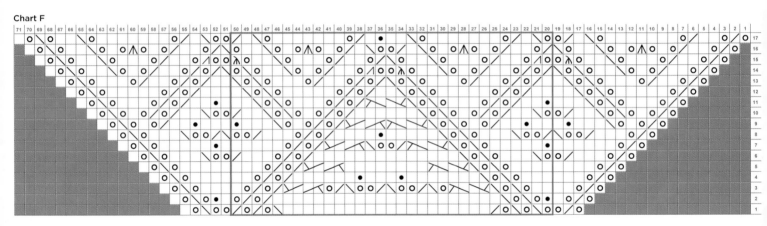

AINNIR

by Luise O'Neill

FINISHED MEASUREMENTS
12.25 (18.75, 25.25)" wide x 70" long.

YARN
Knit Picks Palette (100% Peruvian Highland Wool; 231 yards/50g): Bluebell 24578, 3 (5, 6) balls.

NEEDLES
US 5 (3.75mm) straight or circular needles, or size to obtain gauge

NOTIONS
Yarn Needle
Cable Needle
Scrap Yarn and Crochet Hook, or as preferred for provisional CO

GAUGE
18 sts = 3.25" and 26 rows = 3.5" over Chart A lace pattern repeat, blocked.

Ainnir

Notes:

Ainnir begins with a provisional cast on at the center back and is worked outward toward one end. The main lace pattern (Chart A) is worked seven times before the end border (Chart B) is added. The provisionally cast on stitches are then picked up and the second half is worked as the first.

Read charts on RS rows (odd numbers) from right to left, and WS rows (even numbers) from left to right.

1 over 1 over 1 Right Purl Twist (1/1/1 RPT): Sl next 2 sts to CN and place at back of work, K1 TBL, sl left-most st from CN to LN, move CN with remaining st to front of work, P1 from LN, then K1 TBL from CN.

Make 1 (M1): Lift yarn between the needles, from front to back, and knit into back of lifted loop. 1 st inc.

DIRECTIONS

Provisionally CO 69 (105, 141) sts.

Setup Row (WS): Purl.

Side 1

Work Rows 1 – 26 of Chart A Main Pattern, working sts between red borders 1 (3, 5) time(s).

Rep the 26 rows of Chart A 6 more times.

Work Rows 1 – 65 of Chart B End Border, working sts between red borders 1 (3, 5) time(s).

Row 66 (WS): Sl 1, P to end.

Row 67: Sl 1, *YO, K2tog; rep from * to end.

Rows 68 – 69: Rep Row 66.

With WS facing, BO loosely in purl.

Cut yarn leaving a 6" tail.

Side 2

Transfer 68 (104, 140) provisionally CO sts to needle, ready to work a WS row (due to the nature of a provisional CO, when the sts are unzipped one less st will be on the needles).

Setup Row (WS): Sl 1, M1, P1, K1, P1, (K1, P1 TBL) 2 times, K1, P13, K1, P1 TBL, K1, *P1 TBL, K1, P13, K1, P1 TBL, K1; rep from * 0 (2, 4) times, P1 TBL, K1, P13, (K1, P1 TBL) 2 times, (K1, P1) 2 times, K2. 69 (105, 141) sts.

Continue as for Side 1.

Finishing

Weave in ends. Wash and block to measurements; for the ends, pin only sts at both outer edges and sts at repeat lines on Chart B, pulling them into points.

Chart A

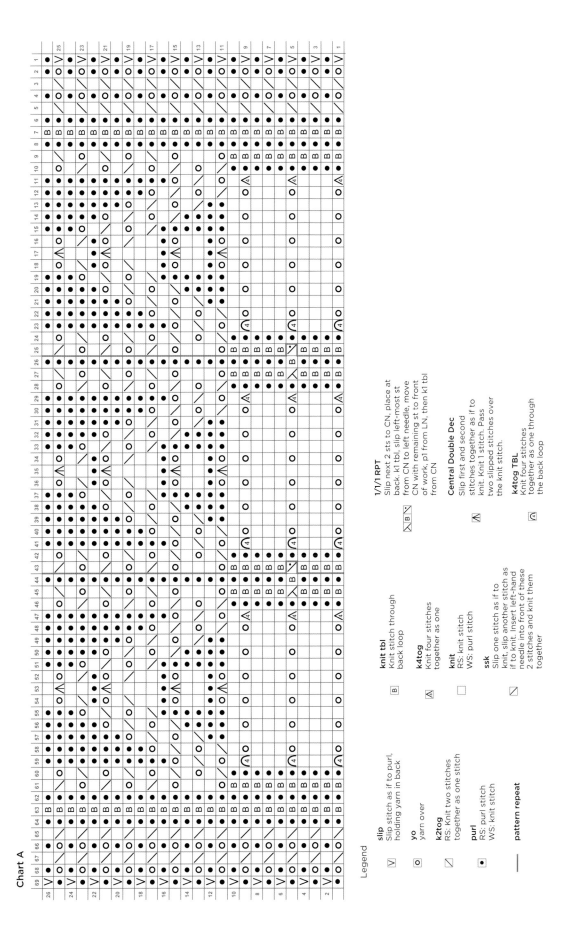

Legend

slip
☑ Slip stitch as if to purl, holding yarn in back

yo
◯ yarn over

k2tog
╱ RS: Knit two stitches together as one stitch

purl
• RS: purl stitch
WS: knit stitch

— **pattern repeat**

knit tbl
B Knit stitch through back loop

k4tog
Ⓐ Knit four stitches together as one

knit
☐ RS: knit stitch
WS: purl stitch

ssk
╱ Slip one stitch as if to knit, slip another stitch as if to knit. Insert left-hand needle into front of these 2 stitches and knit them together

1/1 RPT
Slip next 2 sts to CN, place at back. k1 tbl, slip left-most st from CN to left needle, move CN with remaining st to front of work, p1 from LN, then k1 tbl from CN

Central Double Dec
Slip first and second stitches together as if to knit. Knit 1 stitch. Pass two slipped stitches over the knit stitch.

k4tog TBL
Ⓐ Knit four stitches together as one through the back loop

Chart B

KERTI SHAWL

by Heddi Craft

FINISHED MEASUREMENTS

25" back depth, 42" wide at widest point

YARN

Knit Picks Gloss Lace (70% Merino Wool, 30% Silk; 440 yards/50g): Sterling 24182, 2 hanks.

NEEDLES

US 5 (3.75mm) 36" or longer circular needles, or size to obtain gauge

NOTIONS

Yarn Needle
Stitch Markers
Removable Stitch Markers

GAUGE

21 sts and 32 rows = 4" in St st, blocked.
(Gauge for this project is approximate)

Kerti Shawl

Notes:

This pattern is worked from the bottom up using a long, stretchy cast on. The bottom border of points is created using a series of charted short rows for each point. The body of the shawl is worked from charts in pairs of two, one for the side panels and another for the center panel. A garter stitch edge is knitted on to the top of the center panel.

Notes are added throughout the pattern to provide additional details for certain construction techniques and hints for working more effectively.

The pattern includes nupps to add texture and patterning to the shawl. These could be omitted or replaced with beads if desired. Location of the nupps is indicated by a pair of stacked K1into5 and P5tog symbols on the chart. When working the charts, read RS rows (odd numbers) from right to left, and WS rows (even numbers) from left to right.

Nupps

K1into5 (Knit 1 into 5): K1 but do not remove st from left needle, (YO, K1) into same st twice, remove st from left needle (work sts very loosely for this pattern, to facilitate the P5tog). 5 sts.

P5tog: Sl needle as if to P through next 5 sts, draw yarn through and drop sts from left needle, adjust tension as needed. 4 sts dec, nupp created.

DIRECTIONS

Set Up

CO 369 sts using a method that creates a stretchy cast on. Suggested cast ons include a cable CO, a loop CO, or use a two ball long tail CO.

Note: Placing markers as part of the CO process will assist in knitting the first two charts of short rows and simplify the amount of counting needed. Place markers as follows. CO 5 sts, PM, (CO 37 sts, PM) 4 times, CO 63 sts, PM, (CO 37 sts, PM) 4 times, CO 5 sts.

Pointed Edging

Note: 5 border sts worked in Garter st at either end of the knitting form the top edge of the shawl. The four shorter points on each side of the shawl are created using Chart A and the larger center point is created using Chart B. If you placed markers, you will notice that you will knit across about half of the sts between two markers on Row 1 of either Chart A or B. You will turn your work for Row 2 and work the chart back over only a few sts, turn, work across the next row of the chart, and so on. Each row of the chart uses one additional st until at the end of the last row of the chart you have reached the next stitch marker.

Do not wrap any sts for the short rows. Simply turn the work and begin the next row of the chart. The small holes formed will become part of the pattern.

Pointed Edging

Knit 4 rows.

K5, SM (if using).

Work Rows 1-33 of Chart A over next 37 sts, SM's as you go. Repeat 3 more times.

Work Rows 1-59 of Chart B one time.

Work Rows 1-33 of Chart A over next 37 sts.

Repeat 3 more times. After final chart row SM, K5. 351 sts (count nupp loops as one st).

Note: Chart A includes the beginning of a nupp in Row 33. Nupps are elongated bobble sts that add texture to the knitting. Work 5 sts very loosely into st indicated and place a removable marker through the five loops to both hold some of their looseness in place and to mark their position when working them together again as the P5tog on the WS. Remove these markers when you complete the final WS row.

In the final WS row of this section (next instruction), you will purl the first st from each chart together with the last st from the previous chart except at the five st garter border on either side. This will unify the the knitting between the points and adjust the st count as you begin the body of the shawl. If you used markers, you will remove them as you work the P2tog sts.

Next Row (WS): Removing markers as you go, K5, P1, *P16, P5tog (nupp created), P16, P2tog; rep from * 3 more times, P59, P2tog, *P16, P5tog (nupp created), P16, P2tog; rep from * two more times, P16, P5tog (nupp created), P17, K5. 343 sts.

Charts C1 and C2

Note: In the C1 chart, you will begin to close up the lace diamonds. If you are "reading" your lace, you will notice that the yarnovers start to move inward instead of outward.

Row 1: K5, PM, work Row 1 of Chart C1, PM, work Row 1 of Chart C2, PM, work Row 1 of Chart C1 again, PM, K5.

Row 2: K5, P across working any sts indicated on Row 2 of Chart C1, C2, then C1 again, and SM's to last M, K5.

Row 3: K5, SM, work Row 3 of Chart C1, SM, work Row 3 of Chart C2, SM, work Row 3 of Chart C1 again, SM, K5.

Continue as established through Row 14 of Charts C1 and C2. 315 sts.

Charts D1 and D2

Row 1: K5, SM, work Row 1 of Chart D1, SM, work Row 1 of Chart D2, SM, work Row 1 of Chart D1 again, SM, K5.

Row 2: K5, P across working any sts indicated on Row 2 of Chart D1, D2, then D1 again, and SM's to last M, K5.

Row 3: K5, SM, work Row 3 of Chart D1, SM, work Row 3 of Chart D2, SM, work Row 3 of Chart D1 again, SM, K5.

Continue as established through Row 28 of Charts D1 and D2. 259 sts.

Charts E1 and E2

Row 1: K5, SM, work Row 1 of Chart E1, SM, work Row 1 of Chart E2, SM, work Row 1 of Chart E1 again, SM, K5.

Row 2: K5, P across working any sts indicated on Row 2 of Chart E1, E2, then E1 again, and SM's to last M, K5.

Row 3: K5, SM, work Row 3 of Chart E1, SM, work Row 3 of Chart E2, SM, work Row 3 of Chart E1 again, SM, K5.

Continue as established through Row 28 of Charts E1 and E2. 203 sts.

Chart F

Row 1: K5, SM, YO, Sssk, K to last 3 sts before next M, K3tog, YO,

SM, work Row 1 of Chart F, SM, YO, Sssk, K to last 3 sts before next M, K3tog, YO, SM, K5. 199 sts.

Row 2: K5, P across and working any sts indicated on Row 2 of Chart F and SM's to last M, K5.

Row 3: K5, SM, YO, Sssk, K to last 3 sts before next M, K3tog, YO, SM, work Row 3 of Chart F, SM, YO, Sssk, K to last 3 sts before next M, K3tog, YO, SM, K5. 195 sts.

Continue as established through Row 62 of Chart F. 65 sts.

Row 63: K5, SM, YO, Sl 2, K3tog, p2sso, YO, SM, K to next M, SM, YO, Sl 2, K3tog, p2sso, YO, SM, K5. 61 sts.

Row 64: K5, P across to last 5 sts, K5.

Row 65: K5, SM, K3tog, SM, K45, SM, K3tog, SM, K5. 57 sts.

Row 66: K5, P across to last 5 sts removing markers as you go, K5.

Garter Border

Note: On your needles from right to left you will see the 5 st right garter border, one st that forms the point of the right triangular panel, the 45 sts across the top of the center panel, one st that forms the point of the left triangular panel, and 5 garter sts for the left garter border. These directions use short rows to create the rest of the garter border perpendicular to the center panel and attach it to the shawl at the same time. The RS row in the directions will pick up additional sts from the center panel each time it is worked and the WS row will return the knitter to the edge of the work.

Row 1 (RS): K5, K2tog, turn.
Row 2 (WS): Sl 1 P-wise WYIB, YO, K2tog, K3, turn.
Row 3: K5, K2tog, turn.

Repeat Rows 2 and 3 until 12 sts remain, ending with a WS row. Cut yarn leaving a long tail threaded on a yarn needle. Place 6 sts on each of two needles and graft them together using Kitchener st with WS of shawl touching and RS facing out.

Finishing

Weave in ends, wash and block to diagram, pulling out points with blocking wires or pins.

Chart A

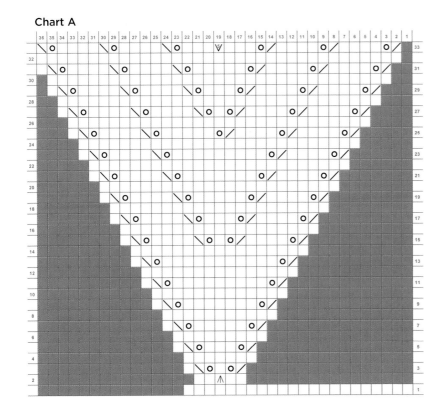

Legend

knit
RS: knit stitch
WS: purl stitch

No Stitch
Placeholder - No stitch made.

central double decrease
RS: slip 2 sts, knit 1, pass 2 slipped stitches over knit st
WS: slip 2 sts purlwise, purl 1, pass 2 slipped stitches over purl st

k2tog
RS: Knit two stitches together as one stitch
WS: Purl 2 stitches together

yo
yarn over

ssk
Slip one stitch as if to knit,
Slip another stitch as if to knit.
Insert left-hand needle into front of these 2 stitches and knit them together

k3tog
Knit three stitches together as one

m5 sts in one
(k1 yo k1 yo k1) in one stitch

p5tog
Purl five stitches together as one

sssk
(Slip 1 as if to knit) 3 times;
insert left-hand needle from the front to the back of all stitches at the same time and knit them together.

Chart B

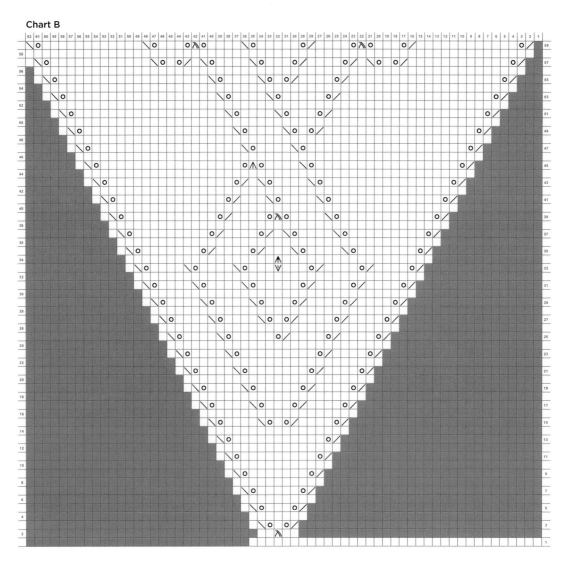

Chart C1

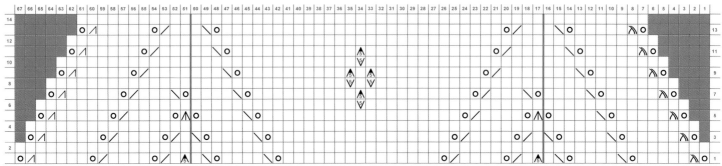

Work area between the red lines three times.

Chart C2

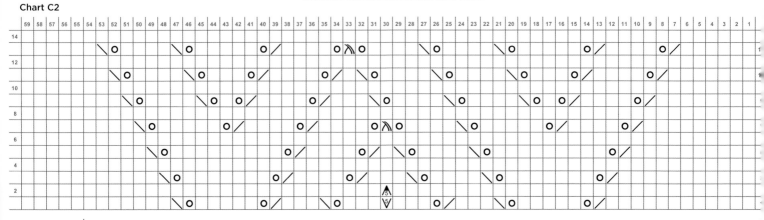

Chart D1

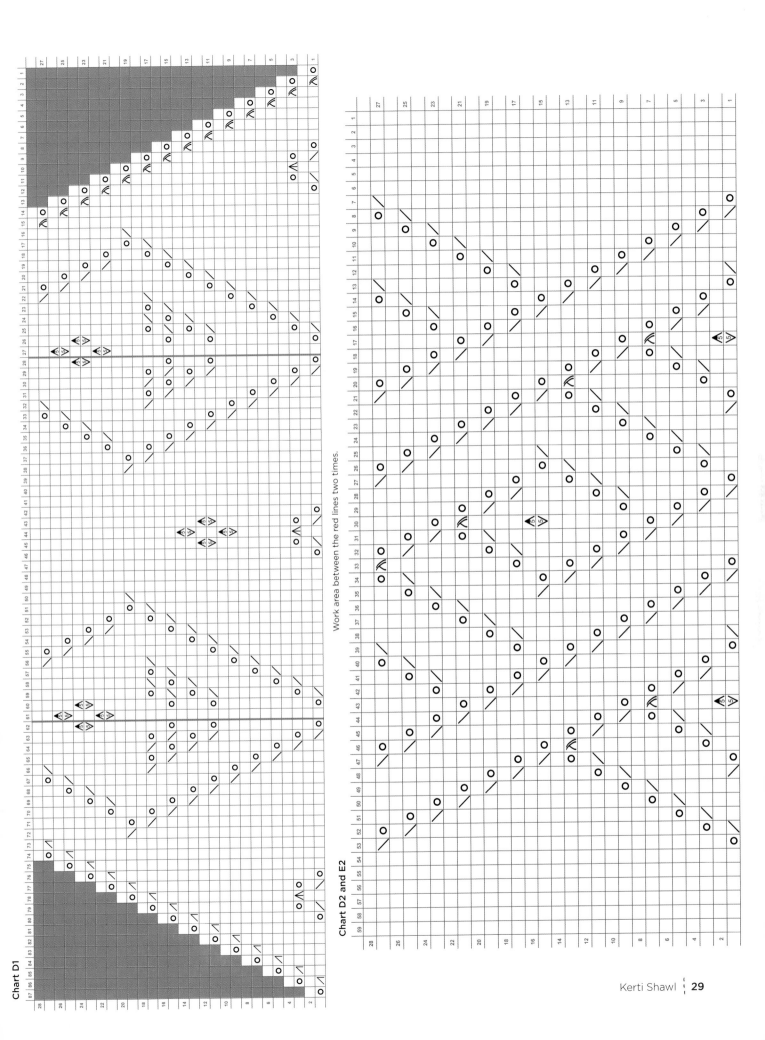

Work area between the red lines two times.

Chart D2 and E2

Chart E1

Chart F

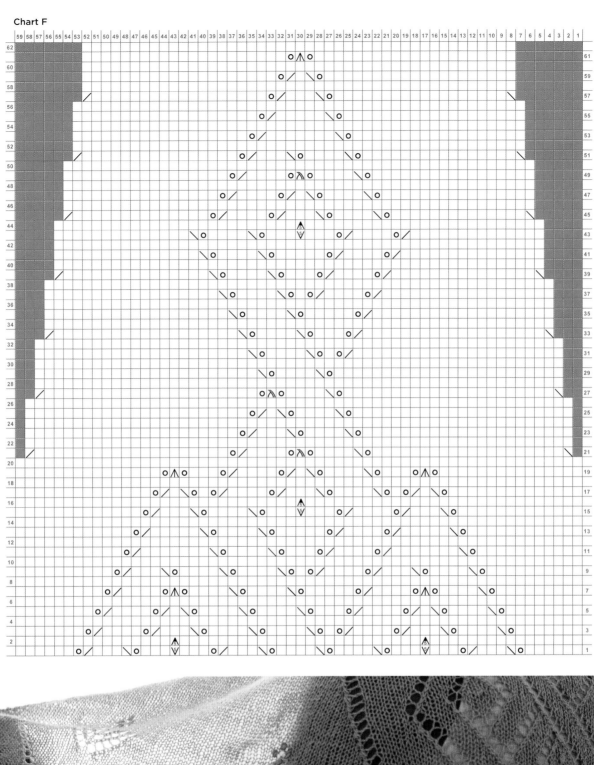

AUSTEN

by Kirsten Singer

FINISHED MEASUREMENTS
27" wide x 68" long

YARN
Knit Picks Luminance (100% Silk; 878 yards/100g): Bare 27059, 2 skeins

NEEDLES
US 3 (3.25mm) straight or short circular needles, plus 40" or longer circular needle or size to obtain gauge

NOTIONS
Yarn Needle
Stitch Markers
Crochet Hook and Smooth Waste Yarn, or as preferred for Provisional CO

GAUGE
17 sts and 34 rows = 4" over Austen Lace Pattern, blocked.

Austen

Notes:

The body of the scarf begins with a provisional cast on and is knit to the desired length, and stitches are placed on a circular needle. Then, stitches for the edging are picked up evenly around the body of the shawl, and the provisional cast on is removed and these stitches are placed on the circular needle. The edging is knit on to the live stitches on the circular needle. Follow the charts from right to left on RS rows (odd numbers) and left to right on WS rows (even numbers).

Austen Lace Pattern (worked flat over multiples of 8 sts plus 10)

Row 1 (RS): K3, SSK, YO, K2 *YO, SSK, K2, SSK, YO, K2; rep from * to last 3 sts, K3.

Row 2 and all even rows through Row 8 (WS): K3 *P2tog, YO, P6; rep from * to last 7 sts, P2tog, YO, P2, K3.

Row 3: K3, SSK, YO, K2 *K1, YO, SSK, K1, SSK, YO, K2; rep from * to last 3 sts, K3.

Row 5: K3, SSK, YO, K2 *K2, YO, SSK twice, YO, K2; rep from * to last 3 sts, K3.

Row 7: K3, SSK, YO, K2 *K3, YO, SK2P, YO, K2; rep from * to last 3 sts, K3.

Rep Rows 1-8 for pattern.

Austen Edging (worked flat)

Row 1 (RS): Sl 1, K2, YO, K2tog, K3, YO, K2tog, K2, YO, K2tog, YO, K2.

Row 2 and all even rows through 16 (WS): P to last 3 sts, YO, K2tog edging join.

Row 3: Sl 1, K2, YO, K2tog, K2, (YO, K2tog)2x, K2, YO, K2tog, YO, K2.

Row 5: Sl 1, K2, YO, K2tog, K3, (YO, K2tog)2x, K2, YO, K2tog, YO, K2.

Row 7: Sl 1, K2, YO, K2tog, K2, (YO, K2tog)3x, K2, YO, K2tog, YO, K2.

Row 9: Sl 1, K2, YO, K2tog, K2, (K2tog, YO)2x, K2, (K2tog, YO)2x, K2tog, K1.

Row 11: Sl 1, K2, YO, K2tog, K1, (K2tog, YO)2x, K2, (K2tog, YO)2x, K2tog, K1.

Row 13: Sl 1, K2, YO, K2tog, K2, K2tog, YO, K2, (K2tog, YO)2x, K2tog, K1.

Row 15: Sl 1, K2, YO, K2tog, K1, K2tog, YO, K2, (K2tog, YO)2x, K2tog, K1.

Rep Rows 1-16 for pattern.

Edging Join (WS): Knit last st of edging to next live st from center panel, turn.

DIRECTIONS

Center Panel

Using a provisional cast on method, CO 80 sts.

Using shorter needles, work Garter st (K every row) for 4 rows.

Begin working Austen Lace Pattern Rows 1 – 8, repeating until scarf measures 60", or desired length.

Work 4 rows in Garter st. Place these live sts on longer circular needle.

Edging

Using the same circular needle, PM, then PU 1 st in each Garter st ridge along one side of center panel (one st for every 2 rows worked). Continue as established until you reach your provisional CO edge. PM, and remove the provisional CO and place these sts on the circular needle. Place a 3rd marker, and PU sts evenly along other side of the panel, as before. Total st count varies with the length of the scarf.

Lace Edging

Note: The last edging st of every WS row will be worked together with one live st from around the center panel by a K2tog, this joins the edging to the center panel as you go.

CO 16 sts.

Work Rows 1-16 of Lace Edging Chart until you reach 2 sts before your first marker.

Turn the Corner

Continue working chart as established, but omit the edging join, and just knit that st on every other RS row – you will be working 16 Lace Edging rows over the next 4 sts as opposed to 8 rows, to provide ease around the corner.

Return to working Lace Edging chart as established, working the remaining 3 corners as directed above. Once all corners have been turned, BO edging sts and seam to edging CO sts.

Finishing

Wet-block scarf to measurements in schematic. It's highly recommended that you use blocking wires to accentuate the lace points of the scarf's edging. Weave in all ends.

Austen Edging

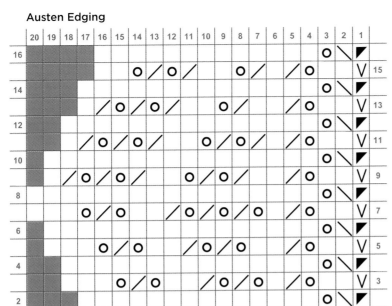

Austen Lace Pattern Chart

Row	18	17	16	15	14	13	12	11	10	9	8	7	6	5	4	3	2	1
8	●	●	●	/	O							/	O			●	●	●
7						O	Λ	O					O	\				
6	●	●	●	/	O								O	\		●	●	●
5						O	\	\	O				O	\				
4	●	●	●	/	O							/	O			●	●	●
3						O	\			\	O		O	\				
2	●	●	●	/	O								O			●	●	●
1					O	\			\	O			O	\				

Legend

slip
RS: Slip stitch as if to purl, holding yarn in back
WS: Slip stitch as if to purl, holding yarn in front

knit
RS: knit stitch
WS: purl stitch

yo
yarn over

k2tog
RS: Knit two stitches together as one stitch
WS: Purl 2 stitches together

No Stitch
Placeholder - No stitch made.

k2tog last st of edging to st from center panel

ssk
RS: Slip one stitch as if to knit, slip another stitch as if to knit. Insert left-hand needle into front of these 2 stitches and knit them together
WS: Purl two stitches together in back loops, inserting needle from the left, behind and into the backs of the 2nd & 1st stitches in that order

Central Double Dec
Slip first and second stitches together as if to knit. Knit 1 stitch. Pass two slipped stitches over the knit stitch.

pattern repeat

AURELIA

by Jenny Williams

FINISHED MEASUREMENTS

24 x 69", including top and bottom edging

YARN

Knit Picks Shadow Lace Yarn (100% Merino Wool; 440 yards/50g): Opal Heather 25366, 4 hanks.

NEEDLES

US 3 (3.25mm) 32" circular needles, or size to obtain gauge

NOTIONS

Crochet Hook
Yarn Needle
Stitch Markers
Cable Needle
Smooth Waste Yarn, worsted weight
Blocking Wires

GAUGE

23 sts and 38 rows = 4" over Falling Leaves chart, blocked.

Aurelia

Notes:

The body of this rectangular lace stole is knitted flat with a fixed stitch count, making it a relatively easy lace project. It features a lattice border along the outer edges and five openwork leaf patterns, each separated by a 4 stitch cable twist for added texture. The leaf patterns are designed to flow both upwards and downwards, eliminating a "wrong" direction as you wear it. A lace edging is knitted sideways into the top and bottom edges, for a seamless finish.

Provisional Cast On

With waste yarn and the crochet hook, crochet a chain a few sts longer than the number of required CO sts. Break waste yarn. Using project yarn and the circular needle, pick up a st into the "bump" on the back of each chain st for the number of CO sts needed, leaving a few "bumps" unworked at each end.

DIRECTIONS

Using the Provisional Cast On method, CO 140 sts.
Purl 1 row, decreasing 2 sts evenly across row. 138 sts.

Body

Charts are worked from right to left on the RS (odd numbered rows) and from left to right on the WS (even numbers).

Using markers to separate charts if desired, work charts as follows: Right Lattice Border, Falling Leaves, 4st Cable with Eyelet Edge, Climbing Leaves, 4st Cable with Eyelet Edge, Falling Leaves, 4st Cable with Eyelet Edge, Climbing Leaves, 4st Cable with Eyelet Edge, Falling Leaves, Left Lattice Border.

Continue working charts as established for 50.5 repeats of the Leaves Charts, ending with Row 6 of Falling Leaves and Climbing Leaves Chart, increasing 2 sts evenly across the final row. 140 sts total. Leave Body on needles.

Knitted Lace Edging

With RS facing, CO 7 sts using knitted cast on method.
Work Row 1 of Zigzag Edging Chart over these 7 sts, purling last CO st tog with first st of body.
Turn and work Row 2 of Zigzag Edging Chart.
Continue working Zigzag Edging, purling last RS row st tog with next Body st each time.
Repeat Zigzag Edging Chart 20 times.
Bind off.

Remove waste yarn and place resulting 140 live sts on circular needles. Repeat Knitted Lace Edging instructions.

Finishing

Weave in ends and block using lace blocking wires.

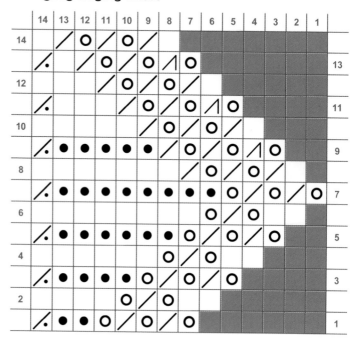

4 st Cable with Eyelet Edge Chart

	10	9	8	7	6	5	4	3	2	1	
4	●									●	
	●	\	O	\		/		O	/	●	3
2	●									●	
	●	\	O					O	/	●	1

Zigzag Edging Chart

	14	13	12	11	10	9	8	7	6	5	4	3	2	1	
14	/	O	/	O	/										
	/•		/	O	/	O	/	∧	O						13
12			/	O	/	O	/								
	/•		/	O	/	O	/	∧	O						11
10				/	O	/	O	/							
	/•	●	●	●	●	●	/	O	/	O	∧	O			9
8					/	O	/	O	/						
	/•	●	●	●	●	●	●	O	/	O	/	O			7
6						O	/	O	/						
	/•	●	●	●	●	●	O	/	O	/	O				5
4					O	/	O	/							
	/•	●	●	●	O	/	O	/	O						3
2				O	/	O	/								
	/	●	●	O	/	O	/	O							1

P2tog with first edge st of shawl body

Climbing Leaves Chart

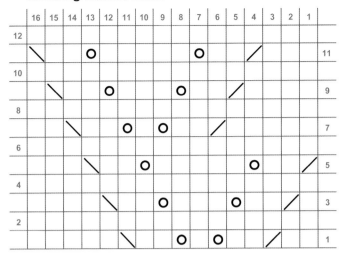

Falling Leaves Chart

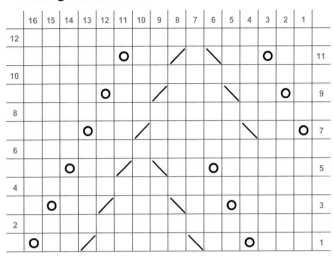

Right Lattice Border Chart

Row 1: yarn is pulled from the back of work and in front of st 1, which is slipped

Left Lattice Border Chart

Row 1: yarn is pulled from the front of work and in front of st 1, which is slipped and to the back

Legend

knit
RS: knit stitch
WS: purl stitch

k2tog
RS: Knit two stitches together as one stitch
WS: Purl 2 stitches together

yo
yarn over

ssk
Slip one stitch as if to knit, slip another stitch as if to knit. Insert left-hand needle into front of these 2 stitches and knit them together

No Stitch
Placeholder - No stitch made.

c2 over 2 right
sl2 to CN, hold in back. k2, k2 from CN

purl
RS: purl stitch
WS: knit stitch

slip wyif
Slip stitch as if to purl, with yarn in front

p2tog
Purl 2 stitches together

k3tog
Knit three stitches together as one

HALF-MOON SUMMER SHAWL

by Halleh Tehranifar

FINISHED MEASUREMENTS

Approximately 23" deep from center back neck down and 54" across widest part.

YARN

Knit Picks Palette (100% Peruvian Highland Wool; 231 yards/50g): Clematis Heather 24013, 4 skeins.

NEEDLES

US 5 (3.75mm) 36" or longer circular needles, or size to obtain gauge
US 6 (4mm) 36" or longer circular needles, or one size larger than gauge needle

NOTIONS

Yarn Needle
Stitch Markers

GAUGE

23 sts and 40 rows = 4" over Garter Stitch using smaller needles.

Half Moon Summer Shawl

Notes:

Shawl is knitted flat from the top neck downward. Correct gauge is not essential for this project so long you are pleased with how the drape and how the stitch patterns look. The shawl is designed to hang loosely over the shoulders and not to overlap in the front. To achieve a slightly larger or smaller finished size; consider using larger or smaller needle sizes.

If using Diamond Lace Charts, follow all chart rows from bottom up, and RS rows (even numbers) from right to left, WS rows (odd numbers) from left to right.

Garter Stitch (worked flat over any number of sts)
All Rows: K.

Eyelet Lace Pattern (over multiples of 2 sts plus 1)
Row 1 (WS): P1, (YO, P2TOG) to end.
Rows 2, 4, 6 (RS): K.
Rows 3: (P2TOG, YO) to last st, P1.
Rows 5: Rep Row 1.
Rep Rows 1-6 for pattern.

Diamond Lace Pattern 1 (over multiples of 8 sts plus 3)
Row 1 & all WS Rows through 11: P.
Row 2 (RS): K3, (YO, K1, SK2P, K1, YO, K3) to end.
Row 4: K4, (YO, SK2P, YO, K5) to last 4 sts of last rep, K4.
Row 6: K1, K2TOG, (K2, YO, K1, YO, K2, SK2P) to last 3 sts of last rep, SSK, K1.
Row 8: K1, K2TOG, (K1, YO, K3, YO, K1, SK2P) to last 3 sts of last rep, SSK, K1.
Row 10: K1, K2TOG, (YO, K5, YO, SK2P) to last 3 sts of last rep SSK, K1.
Row 12: K2, (YO, K2, SK2P, K2, YO, K1) to end, K1.

Diamond Lace Pattern 2 (over multiples of 10 sts plus 3)
Row 1 & all WS Rows through 15: P.
Row 2 (RS): K3, (YO, K2, SK2P, K2, YO, K3) to end.
Row 4: K4, (YO, K1, SK2P, K1, YO, K5) to last 4 sts of last repeat K4.
Row 6: K5, (YO, SK2P, YO, K7) to last 5 sts of last repeat, K5.
Row 8: K1, K2TOG, (K3, YO, K1, YO, K3, SK2P) to last 3 sts of last rep, SSK, K1.
Row 10: K1, K2TOG, (K2, YO, K3, YO, K2, SK2P) to last 3 sts of last rep SSK, K1.
Row 12: K1, K2TOG, (K1, YO, K5, YO, K1, SK2P) to last 3 sts of last rep SSK, K1.
Row 14: K1, K2TOG, (YO, K7, YO, SK2P) to last 3 sts of last rep SSK, K1.
Row 16: K2, (YO, K3, SK2P, K3, YO, K1) to end, K1.

Diamond Lace Pattern 3 (over multiples of 12 sts plus 3)
Row 1 & all WS Rows through 19: P.
Row 2 (RS): K3, (YO, K3, SK2P, K3, YO, K3) to end.
Row 4: K4, (YO, K2, SK2P, K2, YO, K5) to last 4 sts of last rep, K4.
Row 6: K5, (YO, K1, SK2P, K1, YO, K7) to last final 5 sts of last rep, K5.
Row 8: K6, (YO, SK2P, YO, K9) to last final 6 sts of last repeat, K6.
Row 10: K1, K2TOG, (K4, YO, K1, YO, K4, SK2P) to last 3 sts of last

rep, SSK, K1.
Row 12: K1, K2TOG, (K3, YO, K3, YO, K3, SK2P) to last 3 sts of last rep, SSK, K1.
Row 14: K1, K2TOG, (K2, YO, K5, YO, K2, SK2P) to last 3 sts of last rep SSK, K1.
Row 16: K1, K2TOG, (K1, YO, K7, YO, K1, SK2P) to last 3 sts of last rep SSK, K1.
Row 18: K1, K2TOG, (YO, K9, YO, SK2P) to last 3 sts of last rep SSK, K1.
Row 20: K2, (YO, K4, SK2P, K4, YO, K1) to end, K1.

DIRECTIONS

Using Long Tail Cast On method and smaller needle size, CO 7 sts.
Row 1 (WS): KTBL across.
Row 2 and all RS rows through 24: K.
Row 3: K1, (KFB) twice, K1, (KFB) twice, K1. 11 sts.
Row 5: K1, KFB, K to last 2 sts, KFB, K1. 13 sts.
Row 7: K1, (KFB, K1) 5 times, KFB, K1. 19 sts.
Row 9: K.
Row 11: K2, (KFB, K1) 7 times, KFB, K2. 27 sts.
Row 13: K3, KFB, K to last 4 sts, KFB, K3. 29 sts.
Row 15: K4, (KFB, K1) 5 times, K2, KFB, (K1, KFB) 4 times, K4. 39 sts.
Row 17: K5, KFB, K to last 6 sts, KFB, K5. 41 sts.
Row 19: K.
Row 21: K6, KFB, K to last 7 sts, KFB, K6. 43 sts.
Rows 23, 24: K.

First Eyelet Lace Band and Increase

Row 25: K6, (P1, YO) to last 7 sts, P1, K6. 73 sts.
Rows 26-30: Follow Eyelet Lace Pattern Rows 2-6 while continuing working the first and last 6 sts of each row in Garter st.
Row 31: K5, KFB, K to last 6 sts, KFB, K5. 75 sts.
Rows 32-34: K.
Row 35: K7, KFB, K to last 8 sts, KFB, K7. 77 sts.
Row 36: K.

Second Eyelet Lace Band

Row 37-42: Follow Eyelet Lace Pattern Rows 1-6 while continuing working the first and last 8 sts of each row in Garter st.
Row 43: K7, KFB, K to last 8 sts, KFB, K7. 79 sts.
Rows 44-46: K.
Row 47: K9, KFB, K to last 10 sts, KFB, K9. 81 sts.
Row 48: K.

Third Eyelet Lace Band and Increase

Row 49: K10, (P1, YO) to last 11 sts, P1, K10. 141 sts.
Rows 50-54: Follow Eyelet Lace Pattern Rows 2-6 while continuing working the first and last 10 sts of each row in Garter st.
Row 55: K9, KFB, K to last 10 sts, KFB, K9. 143 sts.
Rows 56-58: K.
Row 59: K11, KFB, K to last 12 sts, KFB, K11. 145 sts.
Row 60: K.

Fourth Eyelet Lace Band

Row 61-66: Follow Eyelet Lace Pattern Rows 1-6 while continuing working the first and last 12 sts of each row in Garter st.

Rows 67: K11, KFB, K to last 12 sts, KFB, K11. 147 sts.

Row 68-70: K

Rows 71: K12, KFB, K to last 13 sts, KFB, K12. 149 sts.

Rows 72-76: K.

Set up for Diamond Lace Pattern, and Increase

Row 77: K13, PM, P to last 13 sts, PM, K13.

Row 78: K to M, SM, K2, (YO, K5, YO, K1) to last st before M, K1, SM, K to end. 189 sts.

Diamond Lace Pattern 1

Rows 79-102: Follow Diamond Lace Pattern 1 over 163 sts between markers for a total of 2 repeats; while keeping the first and last 13 sts of each row in Garter st.

Row 103: Rep Row 77, slipping markers.

Row 104: K to M, SM, K2, (YO, K7, YO, K1) to last st before M, K1, SM, K to end. 229 sts.

Diamond Lace Pattern 2

Rows 105-136: Follow Diamond Lace Pattern 2 over 203 sts between markers for a total of 2 repeats; while keeping the first and last 13 sts of each row in Garter st.

Row 137: Rep Row 77, slipping markers.

Row 138: K to M, SM, K2, (YO, K9, YO, K1) to last st before M, K1, SM, K to end. 269 sts.

Diamond Lace Pattern 3

Rows 139-178: Follow Diamond Lace Pattern 3 over 243 sts between markers for a total of 2 repeats; while keeping the first and last 13 sts of each row in Garter st.

Row 179: Rep Row 77, slipping markers.

Lower Edge Border

Switch to larger needle size.

Rows 180-199: K in Garter st.

On the next RS Row: BO loosely across all sts.

Finishing

Weave in the ends and block the shawl to measurements.

Diamond Lace Pattern 1

Legend

•	**purl**	purl stitch
☐	**knit**	knit stitch
O	**yo**	yarn over
⋏	**sl1 k2tog psso**	slip 1, k2tog, pass slip stitch over k2tog
/	**k2tog**	Knit two stitches together as one stitch
\	**ssk**	Slip one stitch as if to knit, Slip another stitch as if to knit. Insert left-hand needle into front of these 2 stitches and knit them together
—	**pattern repeat**	

Diamond Lace Pattern 2

Diamond Lace Pattern 3

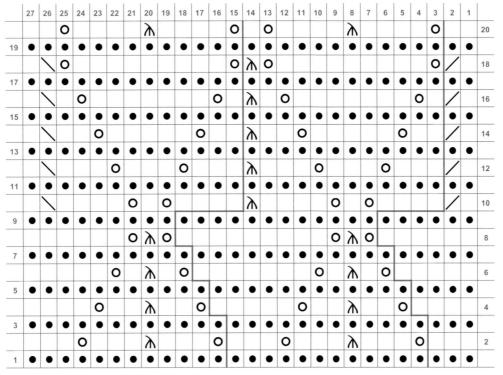

DEWDROP PATHS

by Caroline Steinford

FINISHED MEASUREMENTS

Approximately 40" x 50" (102 x 127 cm)

YARN

Knit Picks Alpaca Cloud Lace (100% Baby Alpaca; 440 yds/50g): Margaret 26784, 1 skein.

NEEDLES

US 4 (3.5mm) 24" or longer circular needles, or size to obtain gauge

NOTIONS

Yarn Needle
Stitch Markers

GAUGE

20 sts and 28 rows = 4" in St st lightly blocked.

Dewdrop Paths

Notes:

Dewdrop Paths is a top-down, curved triangle shawl with an easy lace pattern. It is designed to be simple, but pretty, travel knitting with an easy to memorize stitch pattern. The piece is worked flat with the edging knitted on sideways. The pattern is provided in both charted and written form. The shawl is easily resizable. Just continue repeating to any length. Any weight of yarn may be used, just keep in mind that yardage will change. According to the instructions, the right side of the shawl is the side with the wide columns of purl stitches, but if care is taken weaving in ends, it can be worn reversibly.

Place markers to divide repeats if desired, but try to use distinctive markers to indicate the edge and center stitches.

Read RS chart rows (odd numbers) from right to left, and WS rows (even numbers) from left to right.

Chart A Stitch Pattern

Row 1, Set up (RS): K3, YO, K1, M1, K2tog, YO, P1, YO, SM, K1 , SM, YO, P1, YO, SSK, M1, K1, YO, K3.

Row 2, Set up (WS): K3, P1, K2, P2, K2, SM, P1, SM, K2, P2, K2, P1, K3.

Rows 1 and 2 are only worked on the first pattern repeat.

Row 3: K3, YO, K1, M1, *P2, YO, SSK, P2* to M, YO, SM, K1, SM, YO, *P2, K2tog, YO, P2* to 4 st before end, M1, K1, YO, K3.

Row 4: K3, P1, K2, *K2, P2, K2* to 1 st before M, K1, SM, P1, SM, K1, *K2, P2, K2* to 6 sts before end, K2, P1, K3.

Row 5: K3, YO, K1, M1, P2, *P2, K2tog, YO, P2* to 1 st before M, P1, YO, SM, K1, SM, YO, P1, *P2, YO, SSK, P2* to 6 sts before end, P2, M1, K1, YO, K3.

Row 6: K3, P3, K2, *K2, P2, K2* to 2 sts before M, K2, SM, P1, SM, K2, *K2, P2, K2* to 8 sts before end, K2, P3, K3.

Row 7: K3, YO, K1, M1, YO, SSK, P2, *P2, YO, SSK, P2* to 2 sts before M, P2, YO, SM, K1, SM, YO, P2, *P2, K2tog, YO, P2* to 8 sts before end, P2, K2tog, YO, M1, K1, YO, K3.

Row 8: K3, P1, *K2, P2, K2* to 3 sts before M, K2, P1, SM, P1, SM, P1, K2, *K2, P2, K2* to 4 sts before end, P1, K3.

Row 9: K3, YO, K1, M1, *P2, K2tog, YO, P2* to 3 sts before M, P2, K1, YO, SM, K1, SM, YO, K1, P2, *P2, YO, SSK, P2* to 4 sts before end, M1, K1, YO, K3.

Row 10: K3, P1, K2, *K2, P2, K2* to 4 sts before M, K2, P2, SM, P1, SM, P2, K2, *K2, P2, K2* to 6 sts before end, K2, P1, K3.

Row 11: K3, YO, K1, M1, P2, *P2, YO, SSK, P2* to 4 sts before M, P2, YO, SSK, YO, SM, K1, SM, YO, K2tog, YO, P2, *P2, K2tog, YO, P2* to 6 sts before end, P2, M1, K1, YO, K3.

Row 12: K3, P3, K2, *K2, P2, K2* to 5 sts before M, K2, P2, K1, SM, P1, SM, K1, P2, K2, *K2, P2, K2* to 8 sts before end, K2, P3, K3.

Row 13: K3, YO, K1, M1, K2tog, YO, P2, *P2, K2tog, YO, P2* to 5 sts before M, P2, K2tog, YO, P1, YO, SM, K1, SM, YO, P1, YO, SSK, P2, *P2, YO, SSK, P2* to 8 sts before end, P2, YO, SSK, M1, K1, YO, K3.

Row 14: K3, P1, *K2, P2, K2* to M, SM, P1, SM, *K2, P2, K2* to 4 sts before end, P1, K3.

Repeat Rows 3-14 for pattern.

Chart B Stitch Pattern

Row 1 (RS): Sl1 WYIB, K3, SSK, YO, K3, YO, K1.

Row 2 (WS): K10, K1 tog with live edge st.

Row 3: Sl1 WYIB, K2, SSK, YO, K5, YO, K1.

Row 4: K11, K1 tog with live edge st.

Row 5: Sl1 WYIB, (K1, SSK, YO) twice, K1, YO, K2tog, K1, YO, K1.

Row 6: K12, K1 tog with live edge st.

Row 7: Sl1 WYIB, (SSK, YO, K1) twice, (YO, K2tog) twice, K1, YO, K1.

Row 8: K13, K1 tog with live edge st.

Row 9: Sl1 WYIB, K2, YO, K2tog, K1, YO, (CDD, YO, K1) twice.

Row 10: K12, K1 tog with live edge st.

Row 11: Sl1 WYIB, K3, YO, K2tog, K3, CDD, YO, K1.

Row 12: K11, K1 tog with live edge st.

Row 13: Sl1 WYIB, K4, YO, CDD twice, YO, K1.

Row 14: K9, K1 tog with live edge st.

Row 15: Sl1 WYIB, K5, YO, CDD, YO, K1.

Row 16: K9, K1 tog with live edge st.

Rep Rows 1-16 for pattern.

DIRECTIONS

Garter Tab Cast On

Using backward loop cast on, CO 3 sts.
K 20 rows.
Next Row: K3, PU and K 9 sts along edge, PU and K3 in CO sts. (15 sts)

Body

Setup Row: K3, PM, P4, PM, P1 (center st), PM, P4, PM, K3.

Work Chart A once, then repeat Rows 3-14 six more times or until shawl measures approximately 15.5" (39.5 cm) or desired length at spine, ending with a WS row.
Work one final RS row.

Edge

Please note: The border stitches are CO where the body of the shawl is completed, at the end of a RS row.

With RS facing, CO 10 stitches and K 1 WS row, knitting last CO st tog with first live edge st of shawl. Turn.
Work Chart B, knitting the last st of each even (WS) row tog with the next live st along the shawl edge. Rep Rows 1-16 until one live edge st remains. Work one more RS row. K 1 WS row, knitting last st tog with last live st.
BO K-wise on RS.

Finishing

Weave in ends, wash and block to diagram.

Chart A

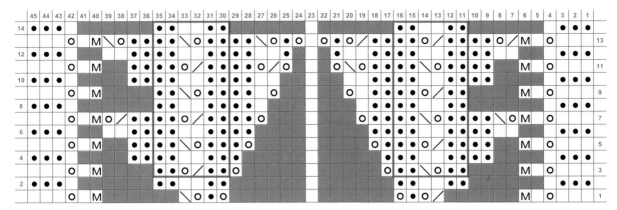

Chart B Edging

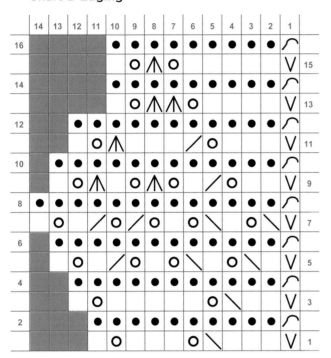

Legend

knit
RS: knit stitch
WS: purl stitch

yo
yarn over

make one
RS: Make one by lifting strand in between stitch just worked and the next stitch, knit into back of this thread.

WS: Make one by lifting strand in between stitch just worked and the next stitch, purl into back of this thread.

No Stitch
Placeholder - no stitch made.

k2tog
RS: Knit two stitches together as one stitch
WS: Purl 2 stitches together

purl
RS: purl stitch
WS: knit stitch

ssk
RS: Slip one stitch as if to knit, Slip another stitch as if to knit. Insert left-hand needle into front of these 2 stitches and knit them together

WS: Purl two stitches together in back loops, inserting needle from the left, behind and into the backs of the 2nd & 1st stitches in that order

pattern repeat

Central Double Dec
Slip first and second stitches together as if to knit. Knit 1 stitch. Pass two slipped stitches over the knit stitch.

slip
Slip stitch as if to purl, holding yarn in back

K1 edge st
Knit 1 stitch together with the edge stitch on WS

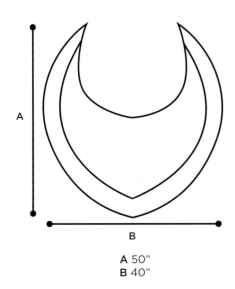

A 50"
B 40"

ESTONIAN WEDDING RING SHAWL

by Geoffrey Hunnicutt

FINISHED MEASUREMENTS

Approximately 72" square

YARN

Knit Picks Gloss Lace (70% Merino Wool, 30% Silk; 440 yards/50g): Bare 24178, 7 skeins

NEEDLES

US 4 (3.5mm) circular needles, or size to obtain gauge

NOTIONS

Stitch Markers
Cable Needles
Yarn Needle

GAUGE

26 sts and 28 rows = 4" over Chart A, blocked.

Estonian Wedding Ring Shawl

Notes:

This wedding ring shawl is started by knitting the center motif flat. After that has been completed, stitches are picked up around the edges and the rest of the shawl is knit in the round.

Stitch markers are used heavily in this pattern. There are many pattern repeats and stitch markers are placed between each one. This enables the knitter to be able to find errors quickly, if any occur.

The even rows have been omitted on all charts. Read the RS rows (odd numbers) from right to left. For Chart A, which is knit flat, all even (WS) row stitches are purl sts. Charts B, C, and D are knit in the round, all even row stitches are knit sts.

In Charts C and D, stitch markers will have to be moved on some rows. This is to keep the stitch counts correct.

Nupps: To knit a nupp, knit into the back of the st, leaving the st on the LH needle, and draw the yarn up loosely. YO loosely, 2 sts on needle. Rep 2 more times, 6 sts on needle. Knit into the back of the st and slip st off LH needle, 7 sts on needle.

Return row/rnd: On WS rows, when working flat, P all 7 nupp sts together. When working in the round, on even rows, K all 7 nupp sts together TBL.

Make 3 from 3: K into the back of the next 3 sts, leaving the sts on the LH needle, YO. K into the back of the same 3 sts, slipping all 3 sts off the needle.

DIRECTIONS
Chart A

CO 114 sts. Begin Chart A. Repeat center pattern repeat 6 times across the row, PM before each pattern repeat. Sl the first and last st of each WS row P-wise.

Continue knitting in pattern as set, knitting Chart A Rows 1-36 5 times.

Knit through Row 18 of Chart A.

Next Row: BO as follows, K2tog TBL. Put the st back on the LH needle. K2tog TBL. Put the st back onto the LH needle and repeat until all sts are BO.

With RS facing, starting on the top edge, *PU 117 sts evenly along the edge of center motif; PM; rep from * along remaining 3 sides. You will have 4 markers at each corner of the shawl. Make the last one a different color to note the beginning of the round. Join to begin working in the rnd. 468 sts.

Chart B

Begin Chart B, working each rnd of the chart individually between the stitch markers. Knit through Row 33, SM's as you come to them.

On Row 34, increase 10 sts evenly along each side. 161 sts per side, 644 sts total.

Chart C

Begin Chart C. There are 7 pattern repeats along each edge. PM before each pattern repeat.

Work rows 1 and 2.

Row 3: *Knit to within 1 st before pattern repeat M. Sl next st to RH needle; remove M. Sl st back onto LH needle and replace M*.

Repeat between * before all pattern repeat markers.

Repeat directions for Row 3 for Rows 5, 7, and 9. You will not need to move markers for the remaining rows of Chart C.

Work all rows of Chart C.

Knit all rows of Chart C again. When you begin Chart C, Row 1 again, you will have enough sts for another pattern repeat. The pattern repeat has also been shifted. Knit to beginning of pattern repeat, PM. *Knit pattern repeat, removing M when you come to it. Knit to beginning of pattern repeat and replace M*. Repeat between * until end of last pattern repeat. Repeat the above directions for the remaining sides.

Knit Rows 3, 5, 7 and 9 as described above.

Repeat Chart C, 3 more times (a total of 4 repeats) following the above directions.

Chart D

Begin Chart D. PM before each pattern repeat.

Knit Rows 1 and 2.

Row 3: *K to within 1 st before pattern rep M. Sl next st to RH needle; remove M. Slip st back onto LH needle and replace M*.

Repeat between * before all pattern repeat markers. Repeat directions for Row 3 for Rows 5, 7, and 9. You will not need to move markers for the remaining rows of Chart D.

Work all rows of Chart D.

BO very loosely as described at the end of Chart A.

Finishing

Wash and block aggressively to open up the lace pattern. Weave in any ends.

Legend

□	**knit** — knit stitch
○	**yo** — yarn over
◩	**ssk** — Slip one stitch as if to knit, Slip another stitch as if to knit. Insert left-hand needle into front of these 2 stitches and knit them together
•	**purl** — purl stitch
◪	**k2tog** — Knit two stitches together as one stitch
⋈	**nupp** — k, yo, k, yo, k, yo, k. Turn and knit these 7 sts together in same stitch
⋉⋈⋊	**Cable 2 Right, Purl 2, Cable 2 Left** — Sl 2 to CN, hold in back. Sl 2 to 2nd CN, hold in front. K2 then P2 from front CN. K2 from back CN
—	**pattern repeat**
B	**knit tbl** — knit stitch through back loop
⋈○⋈	**Make 3 from 3** — Insert needle through the back loops of the next three sts. K1, YO, K1 through the back loops again.
⋌	**sl1, k2tog, psso** — slip 1, k2tog, pass slip stitch over k2tog

Chart A

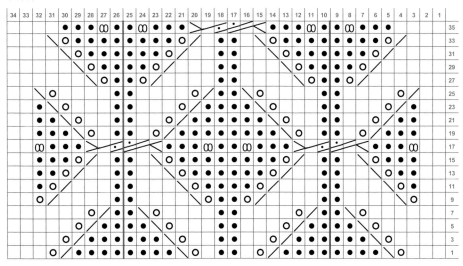

Chart B

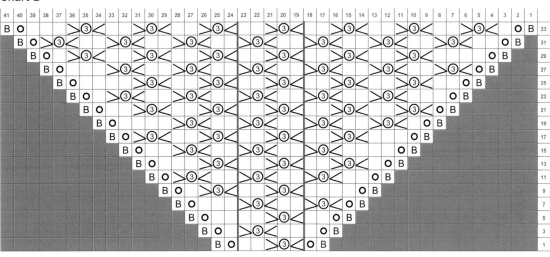

Chart C

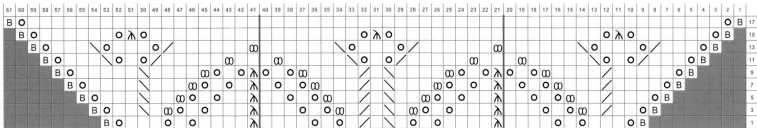

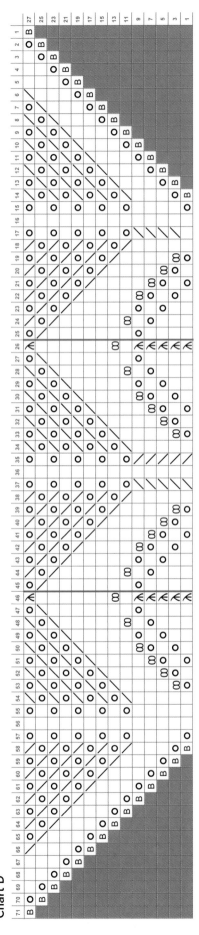

Chart D

THE STOLE OF NESS

by Heather Pfeifer

FINISHED MEASUREMENTS
22" x 59"

YARN
Knit Picks Alpaca Cloud Lace (100% Baby Alpaca; 440 yards/50g): Elinor 26797, 2 skeins.

NEEDLES
US 6 (4mm) straight or circular needles, or size to obtain gauge

NOTIONS
Yarn Needle
2 Stitch Markers
Scrap Yarn
Spare Smaller Needle, for Kitchener Stitch

GAUGE
20 sts x 24 rows = 4" in St st, aggressively wet blocked with lace wires; measurement taken while still on wires.

The Stole of Ness

Notes:

Inspired by Neolithic artwork found at the Ness of Brodgar, this stole features traditional Shetland lace motifs.

The stole begins at the lower edging, where every WS row begins with a YO. The body is worked up from the picked up loops along the edging. Short Rows fill in the mitered corners before beginning the body charts. The LH and RH body edgings are worked simultaneously with the stole body. It is strongly advised to work both pieces at the same time.

The pattern is only charted with the exception of the setup short rows to begin the body. Read RS rows (odd numbers) from right to left, and WS rows (even numbers) from left to right.

Kitchener Stitch

Place held sts onto spare, smaller needle. With an equal number of sts on two needles, break yarn leaving at least 3 times the width of the stole and thread through yarn needle. Hold needles parallel, with WS's facing in and both needles pointing to the right. Perform Step 2 on the first front st, and then Step 4 on the first back st, and then continue with instructions below.
Step 1: Pull yarn needle K-wise through front st and drop st from knitting needle.
Step 2: Pull yarn needle P-wise through next front st, leave st on knitting needle.
Step 3: Pull yarn needle P-wise through first back st and drop st from knitting needle.
Step 4: Pull yarn needle K-wise through next back st, leave st on knitting needle.
Repeat steps 1-4 until all sts have been grafted.
Note: Work YO sts in the same manner as other sts.

German Short Rows

The order of actions with German Short Rows is slightly different than that of common short rows:
(T/W) Turn & Work: Turn piece, yarn to front between needles, Sl 1 st P-wise, pull yarn over right needle to create a Dbl St; continue with Row instructions.
(Dbl st) – Double Stitch: Formed when using the German Short Row method. Knit/Purl both "legs" of the Dbl St together as if a single st.

DIRECTIONS

When both halves of the stole are complete, graft them together using the Kitchener Stitch.

Edging (Make 2)

CO 1 st by making a slip knot.
Note: Chart A Edge Start Row 1 is only the slip knot.
Work Chart A Edge Start once. 9 sts.
Work Chart B Edge Repeat 13 times. 9 sts.
Work Chart C Edge End once. 2 sts.

Do not break yarn.
Total Loops on left edge of each piece, including rem sts on RH needle: 94.

Body

Short Rows (Right Edge)

With RS facing, the YO loops from the LH of the two Edging pieces will now be along the top to begin working the Body.
To pick up loops, insert RH needle from front to back and knit the loop (PU1).

Row 1 (RS): K2. Turn.
Row 2 (WS): P2.
Row 3: K1, YO, K1, PU1. Turn. 4 sts.
Row 4: P4.
Row 5: K1, YO, K3, PU1. Turn. 6 sts.
Row 6: P6.
Row 7: K1, YO, K5, PU1. Turn. 8 sts.
Row 8: P8.
Row 9: SSK, YO, SSK, K1, K2tog, YO, K1, PU1. Turn.
Row 10: P8.
Row 11: SSK, YO, K3tog TBL, YO, K2tog, YO, K1, PU1. Turn.
Row 12: P8.

Next Row (RS): SSK, K1, K2tog, YO, K3, PU 87. 94 sts.

Short Rows (Left Edge)

Note: Purl both legs of the Dbl St together as one st.
Row 1 (WS): P2.
Row 2: T/W, K1.
Row 3: P1, P Dbl St, P1.
Row 4: T/W, K1, YO, K1.
Row 5: P3, P Dbl St, P1.
Row 6: T/W, K3, YO, K1.
Row 7: P5, P Dbl St, P1.
Row 8: T/W, K5, YO, K1.
Row 9: P7, P Dbl St, P1.
Row 10: T/W, K1, YO, SSK, K1, K2tog, YO, K2tog.
Row 11: P7, P Dbl St, P1.
Row 12: T/W, K1, YO, SSK, YO, K3tog TBL, YO, K2tog.
Row 13: P7, P Dbl St, P1.
Row 14: T/W, K3, YO, SSK, K1, K2tog. Total sts: 94 sts. Count the Dbl St as 1 st.
Setup Row (WS): P7, P Dbl St, PM, P2, YO, P36, YO, P36, PM, P2, YO, P10. 97 sts.

Repeat Rows 1-14 and Setup Row (WS) for second piece.

Repeat Rows 1-12 of Chart D 5 times, working sts in red box 5 times. 97 sts.

Work Rows 1-12 of Chart E once, working sts in red box 3 times. 97 sts.

Work Rows 1-12 of Chart F once. 97 sts.

Work Rows 1-12 of Chart G once. 97 sts.
Note: Row 1 (RS) adds two YOs in the center of the row, while Row 2 (WS) has two extra decreases in the center.
Work Rows 1-24 of Chart H at least 3 times, or until desired half length.

If working pieces separately, place live sts of first piece onto scrap yarn. Make second piece.

Finishing

Join two halves using Kitchener Stitch.

Weave in ends, wash and block aggressively with lace wires to diagram.

Legend

No Stitch
RS: Placeholder - No stitch made.

knit
RS: knit stitch
WS: purl stitch

yo
yarn over

ssk
RS: Slip one stitch as if to knit, Slip another stitch as if to knit. Insert left-hand needle into front of these 2 stitches and knit them together
WS: Purl two stitches together in back loops, inserting needle from the left, behind and into the backs of the 2nd & 1st stitches in that order

k2tog
RS: Knit two stitches together as one stitch
WS: Purl 2 stitches together

k3tog tbl
RS: Knit three stitches together through back loops
WS: Purl three stitches together as one, inserting needle from the left and behind

p3tog
WS: Purl three stitches together as one

p2tog tbl
WS: Purl two stitches together through back loop

pattern repeat

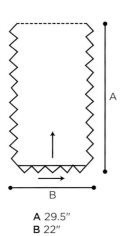

A 29.5"
B 22"

Ness Chart A Edge Start

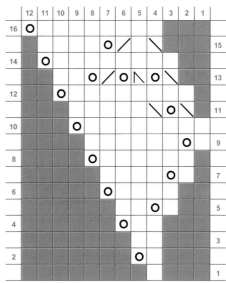

Ness Chart B Edge Repeat

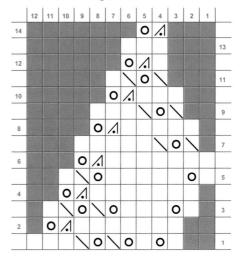

Ness Chart C Edge End

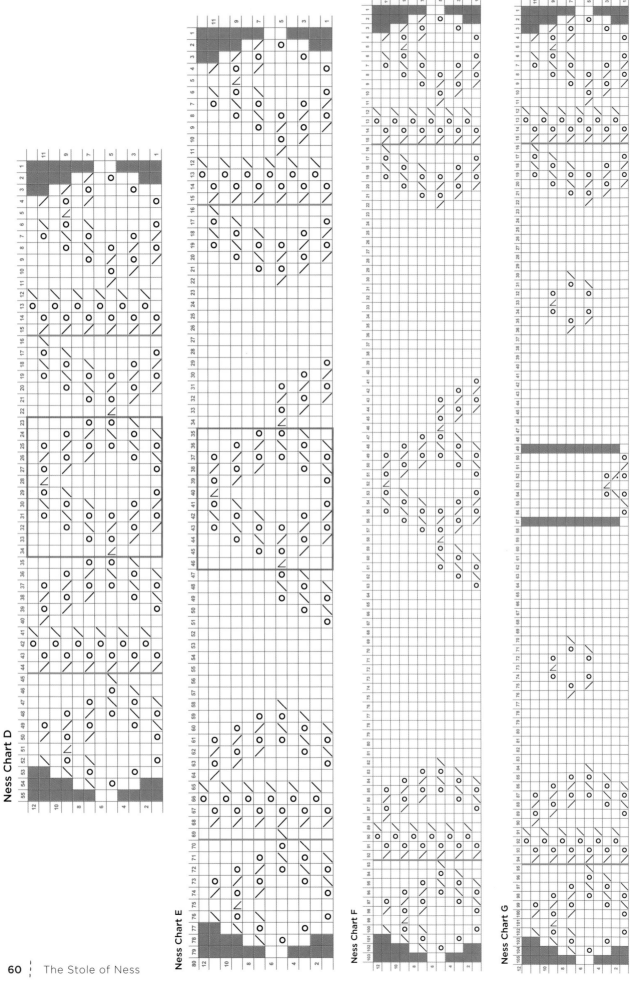

Ness Chart D

Ness Chart E

Ness Chart F

Ness Chart G

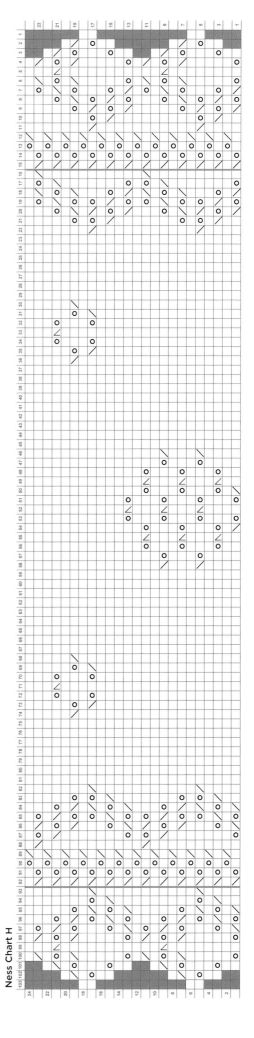

Ness Chart H

ISABEAU

by Stephannie Tallent

FINISHED MEASUREMENTS

15.75" tall at edge; 29.75" tall at center; 77" long at cast on edge; 46.75" long at bind off edge

YARN

Knit Picks Shadow (100% Merino Wool; 440 yards/50g): Oregon Coast 23656, 2 hanks.

NEEDLES

US 2.5 (3.25mm) 32" or longer circular needles, or size to obtain gauge

NOTIONS

Yarn Needle
Stitch Markers as desired

GAUGE

22 sts and 24 rows = 4" over lace pattern, blocked. (Gauge for this project is approximate)

Isabeau

Notes:

This crescent shawl is worked from the bottom up beginning with the lace edging. It's finished with garter stitch short rows.

Only right side rows of the lace edging are charted. Knit the wrong side rows.

When working the chart read RS rows (odd numbers) from right to left.

DIRECTIONS

Loosely CO 424 sts.

Set Up Row (WS): Knit.

Row 1 (RS): Begin Chart Row 1, working the red outlined pattern repeat 11 times.

Row 2 (WS): *K until you reach the double YO, K1 into first loop, KTBL into second loop, repeat from * until last double YO is worked, K to end.

Continue to work RS rows as charted.

Knit all following WS rows (not charted). Complete chart, including last WS row. 339 sts

Short Rows

Row 1 (RS): K178, turn.

Row 2 (WS): Sl1 K-wise, K16, turn.

Row 3: Sl1 K-wise, K to 1 st before turn, SSK, K3, turn.

Repeat last row until you have 1 st remaining on either side of turns.

Next Row (RS): K to 1 st before turn, SSK, turn.

Next Row (WS): K to 1 st before turn, SSK. 257 sts

Last Row (RS): BO K-wise.

Finishing

Wash and block.

Legend

□	**knit**	knit stitch
O	**yo**	yarn over
◻	**ssk**	Slip one stitch as if to knit; slip another stitch as if to knit. Insert left-hand needle into front of these 2 stitches and knit them together
⋏	**sl1, k2tog psso**	slip 1, k2tog, then pass sl stitch over
◻	**k2tog**	knit two stitches together as one stitch
■	**No Stitch**	Placeholder- no stitch made
MR	**make one right**	Place a firm backward loop over the needle, so that the yarn end goes towards the back
◻	**k3tog**	knit three stitches together as one

Isabeau Chart

SHETLAND SHORELINE

by Anne Podlesak

FINISHED MEASUREMENTS
28" Back Neck to Hem x 61" Wingspan

YARN
Knit Picks Palette (100% Peruvian Highland Wool; 231 yards/50g): MC Mist 23733, 3 balls; C1 Silver 24586, 1 ball.

NEEDLES
US 4 (3.5 mm) 36" or longer circular needle, or size to obtain gauge

NOTIONS
Yarn Needle
Stitch Markers

GAUGE
20 sts and 32 rows = 4" over Birds Chart, blocked.

Shetland Shoreline Shawl

Notes:

This shawl is worked from one short end/point of the triangle to the opposite edge, with increases worked along one edge to shape the shawl. Three different lace motifs are worked over the body of the shawl; the first two use only one color, the final one uses a contrast color. The edges are finished with a 2-stitch garter stitch edging.

You may choose to break off and reattach colors in the final lace pattern section, or opt to carry the unused color LOOSELY up the edge of the shawl, catching the unused yarn with the working yarn every other row.

The charts are read from right to left on RS (odd numbered) rows, and left to right on WS (even numbered) rows.

Sl1-K2tog-PSSO: Sl 1 st as if to knit, K2tog, pass slipped st over. 2 sts dec.

Sl2tog-K1-P2SSO: Sl 2 sts tog, K1, pass the 2 slipped sts over. 2 sts dec.

DIRECTIONS

Section One

Using MC, CO 7 sts. Turn work and K7 sts.

Row 1 (RS): K2, PM, KFB, K1, KFB, PM, K2. 9 sts.
Row 2 (WS): K2, SM, P to M, SM, K2.
Row 3: K2, SM, KFB, K3, KFB, SM, K2. 11 sts.
Row 4: Rep Row 2.

When beginning to work the chart, maintain the first and last 2 sts of every row as knit sts to form the garter-stitch edging. These sts are not shown on the charts, but are included in the row stitch counts.

Next Row (RS): K2, SM, work Row 1 of the Shells Chart to last 2 sts, SM, K2.
Continue to work Shells Chart, knitting first and last 2 sts of every row, and working Rows 1-48 of the chart once. (35 sts total; 2 edge sts, 31 shawl sts, 2 edge sts.)

Work Rows 25-48 of the Shells Chart 4 more times. (83 sts; 2 edge sts, 79 shawl sts, 2 edge sts.)

Then work Rows 25-40 of the Shells Chart 1 more time. (91 sts; 2 edge sts, 87 shawl sts, 2 edge sts.)

Section Two

Next Row (RS): K2, SM, work Row 1 of the Birds Chart A to last 2 sts, SM, K2.
Continue to work Birds Chart A, knitting first and last 2 sts of every row. Work chart Rows 1-70 once. (126 sts total; 2 edge sts, 122 shawl sts, 2 edge sts.)

Next Row (RS): K2, SM, work row 1 of the Birds Chart B to last 2 sts, SM, K2.
Continue to work Birds Chart B, knitting first and last 2 sts of every row. Work chart Rows 1-56 once. (154 sts total; 2 edge sts, 150 shawl sts, 2 edge sts.)

Section Three

Next Row (RS): K2, SM, work Row 1 of the Wave Chart to last 2 sts, SM, K2.
Continue to work Wave Chart, knitting first and last 2 sts of every row, switching to the contrast color where indicated, and working Chart Rows 1-76 once. Remove all markers on final row, ending with a WS row. (192 sts total; 2 edge sts, 188 shawl sts, 2 edge sts.)

Knit 2 rows using C1. Break C1.

Then knit 2 rows using MC.

On next row (RS), BO all sts LOOSELY in knit.

Finishing

Weave in ends, wash and block to Finished Measurements, pinning the top and left side edge straight, and pinning the right edge into smooth scallops.

Shells Chart

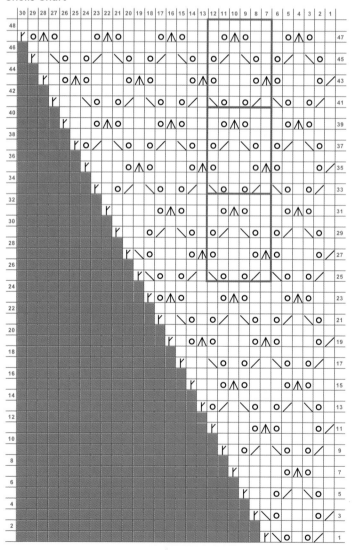

Birds Chart A

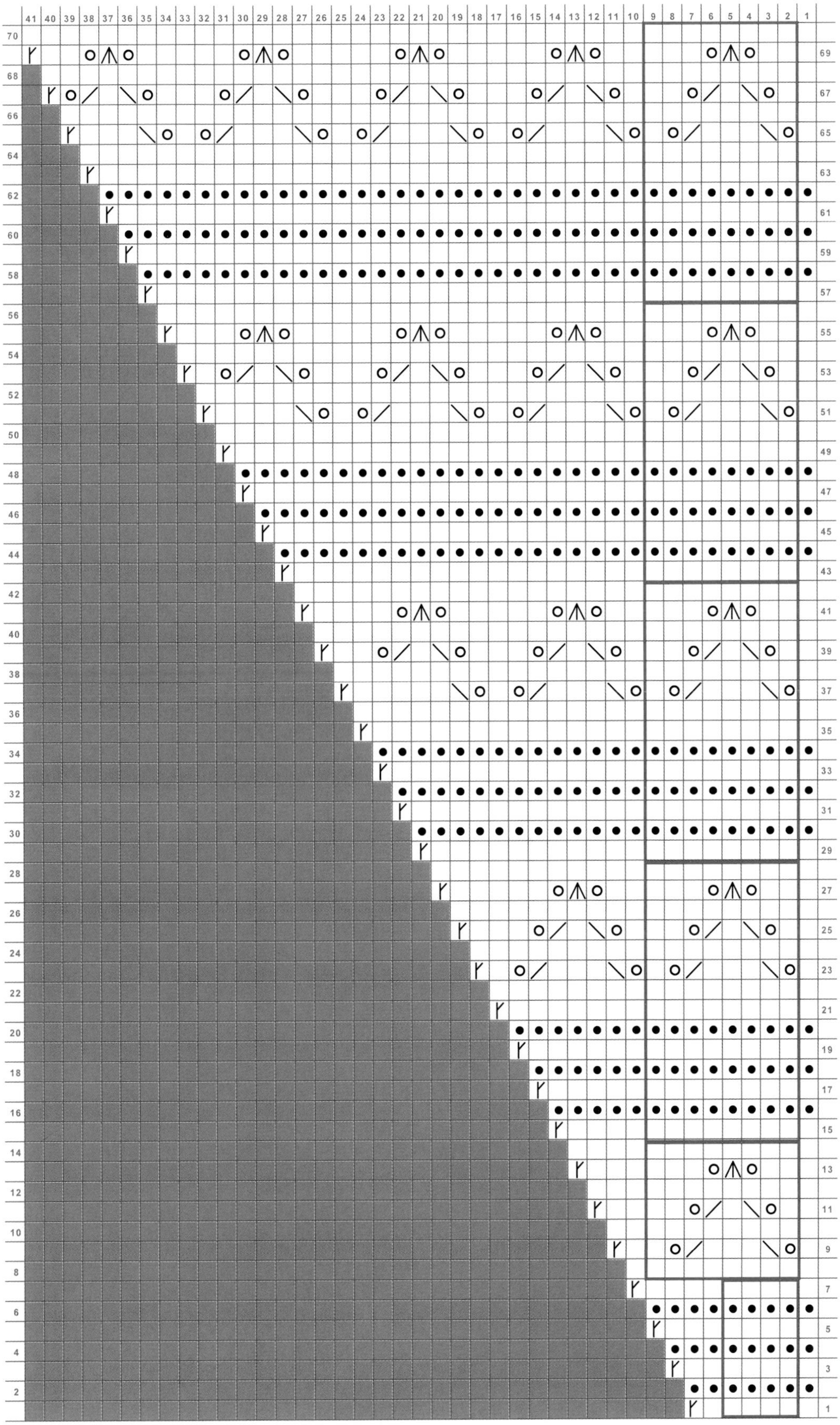

Legend

knit
RS: knit stitch
WS: purl stitch

kfb
RS: Knit into the front and back of the stitch
WS: Purl into the front and the back of the stitch

No Stitch
Placeholder - no stitch made.

purl
RS: purl stitch
WS: knit stitch

yo
yarn over

ssk
RS: Slip one stitch as if to knit, Slip another stitch as if to knit. Insert left-hand needle into front of these 2 stitches and knit them together
WS: Purl two stitches together in back loops, inserting needle from the left, behind and into the backs of the 2nd & 1st stitches in that order

k2tog
RS: Knit two stitches together as one stitch
WS: Purl 2 stitches together

sl2tog, k1, p2sso
RS: Slip first and second stitches together as if to knit. Knit 1 stitch. Pass two slipped stitches over the knit stitch.
WS: Slip first and second stitches as it to purl through the back loop. Purl 1 stitch. Pass two slipped stitches over the purl stitch.

pattern repeat

MC

C1

Birds Chart B

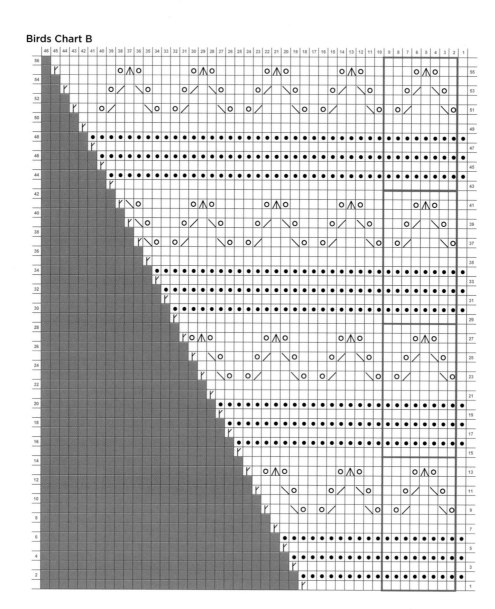

Wave Chart

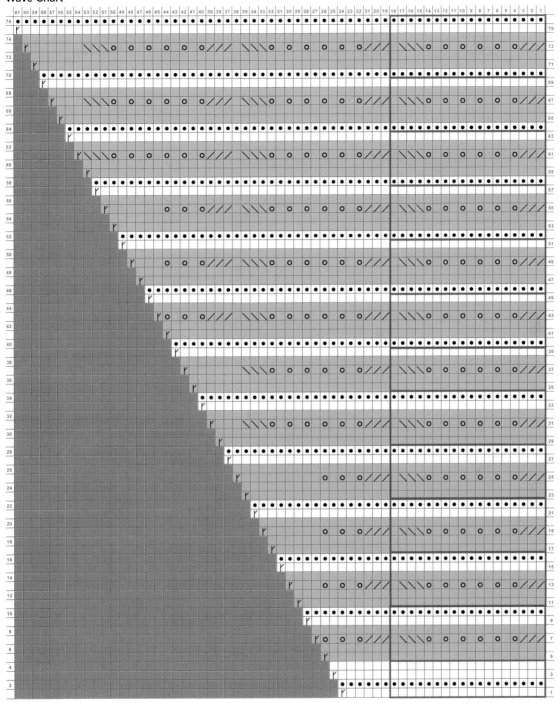

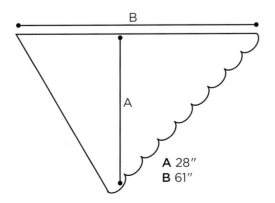

A 28"
B 61"

CYGNUS

by Susanna IC

FINISHED MEASUREMENTS
25" center depth x 63" long

YARN
Knit Picks Aloft (72% Super Kid Mohair, 28% Silk; 260 yards/25g): Sky 25208, 2 balls.

NEEDLES
US 7 (4.5mm) 24" or longer circular needles, or size to obtain gauge

NOTIONS
Yarn Needle
Stitch Markers
Beads (120 4mm 6/0 seed beads, optional)
Crochet Hook (0.75mm, optional, for bead placement only)

GAUGE
20 sts and 26 rows = 4" in Garter stitch, blocked.

Cygnus

Notes:

Inspired by the shapes of the wings of flying birds, Cygnus combines a beautiful traditional Estonian lace pattern with interesting textures in a modern interpretation of a lace wrap. An elongated crescent, this shawl is a versatile addition to any wardrobe; it can be worn loose around the neck as a long scarf or wrapped around the shoulders as a traditional shawl.

This wrap uses an easy construction; it is worked end-to-end in one piece, increasing in width to the half-way point and then decreasing again. Thanks to this construction, this design will accommodate just about any yardage. Cygnus features an easy-to-knit garter stitch body together with a wide lace border, which combines areas of stockinette stitch with garter stitch details and beads for interesting texture. If desired, the beads can be left off or replaced with traditional nupps (to work a nupp, see Bead Placement section).

Bead Placement

To place a bead on a stitch, insert a slender crochet hook through the hole in the bead and slide the bead up onto the hook. Pick the stitch off the needle with the hook and slide the bead down onto the stitch. Slip the stitch back on the left needle and knit it. To skip a bead, simply knit the 'B' stitch. To create a nupp instead of placing a bead, first on RS work (K-YO-K-YO-K-YO-K) into the 'B' stitch (6 sts inc), then on the following WS row purl all seven loops together (one stitch remains).

Make 1 Increase

With left needle, pick up horizontal strand to the left of the last stitch worked, from the front, and knit it through the back loop (twist the stitch). 1 st inc.

Knit TBL

Knit the stitch through the back loop (twist the stitch).

Sl2-K1-PSSO: Slip 2 sts together, K1, pass slipped sts over. 2 sts dec.

Area of Increases and Decreases

These squares in the charts illustrate the Garter stitch area where the stitch count changes according to the increases and decreases along its bottom edge. This area will increase from a single stitch cast on to the widest point at the center of the shawl and then decrease again to a single stitch for bind off. When following the charts, read RS rows (odd numbers) from right to left, and WS rows (even numbers) from left to right.

DIRECTIONS

Cast on 32 sts.
Row 1 (RS): (K4, PM) two times, K17, PM, K4, PM, K3.
Row 2 (WS): Knit to end.
Work Cygnus Increases (Row 1 – 12) fifteen times.
Work Cygnus Decreases (Row 1 – 12) fifteen times.
Knit 2 rows, removing all markers.
Bind off, matching tension of the cast on.

Finishing

Weave in any loose ends. Block to measurements and shape as shown in the blocking schematic. For easier blocking, thread blocking wires through the yarn overs along the top edge and then pin out the lace points created by the double yarn overs along the curved bottom edge. When completely dry, remove pins and trim all yarn tails.

Increases Chart

Columns (left to right): 36 35 34 33 32 31 30 29 28 27 26 25 24 23 22 21 20 19 18 17 16 15 14 13 12 11 10 9 8 7 6 5 4 3 2 1

Rows (right side): 12, 11, 10, 9, 8, 7, 6, 5, 4, 3, 2, 1

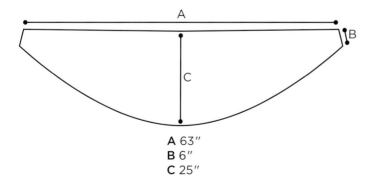

Legend

╱	**k2tog**	knit two stitches together as one stitch
O	**yo**	yarn over
☐	**knit**	RS: knit stitch / WS: purl stitch
M	**make one**	Make one by lifting strand in between stitch just worked and the next stitch, knit into back of this thread.
╲	**ssk**	Slip one stitch as if to knit, Slip another stitch as if to knit. Insert left-hand needle into front of these 2 stitches and knit them together
◆	**bead**	
•	**purl**	RS: purl stitch / WS: knit stitch
B	**knit tbl**	WS: knit stitch through back loop
◼	**bind off 1 st**	
⋀	**Central Double Dec**	slip first and second stitches together as if to knit. Knit 1 stitch. Pass two slipped stitches over the knit st
—	**stitch marker location**	

Decreases Chart

Columns (left to right): 36 35 34 33 32 31 30 29 28 27 26 25 24 23 22 21 20 19 18 17 16 15 14 13 12 11 10 9 8 7 6 5 4 3 2 1

Rows (right side): 12, 11, 10, 9, 8, 7, 6, 5, 4, 3, 2, 1

A
B
C

A 63"
B 6"
C 25"

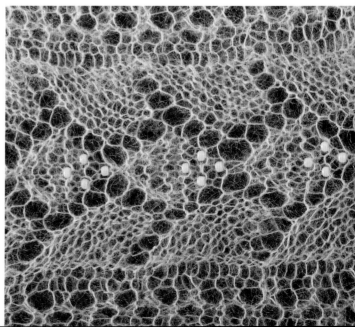

Abbreviations							
BO	bind off	M	marker		stitch	TBL	through back loop
cn	cable needle	M1	make one stitch	RH	right hand	TFL	through front loop
CC	contrast color	M1L	make one left-leaning	rnd(s)	round(s)	tog	together
CDD	Centered double dec		stitch	RS	right side	W&T	wrap & turn (see
CO	cast on	M1R	make one right-lean-	Sk	skip		specific instructions
cont	continue		ing stitch	Sk2p	sl 1, k2tog, pass		in pattern)
dec	decrease(es)	MC	main color		slipped stitch over	WE	work even
DPN(s)	double pointed	P	purl		k2tog: 2 sts dec	WS	wrong side
	needle(s)	P2tog	purl 2 sts together	SKP	sl, k, psso: 1 st dec	WYIB	with yarn in back
EOR	every other row	PM	place marker	SL	slip	WYIF	with yarn in front
inc	increase	PFB	purl into the front and	SM	slip marker	YO	yarn over
K	knit		back of stitch	SSK	sl, sl, k these 2 sts tog		
K2tog	knit two sts together	PSSO	pass slipped stitch	SSP	sl, sl, p these 2 sts tog		
KFB	knit into the front and		over		tbl		
	back of stitch	PU	pick up	SSSK	sl, sl, sl, k these 3 sts		
K-wise	knitwise	P-wise	purlwise		tog		
LH	left hand	rep	repeat	St st	stockinette stitch		
		Rev St st	reverse stockinette	sts	stitch(es)		

Knit Picks yarn is both luxe and affordable—a seeming contradiction trounced! But it's not just about the pretty colors; we also care deeply about fiber quality and fair labor practices, leaving you with a gorgeously reliable product you'll turn to time and time again.

THIS COLLECTION FEATURES

Palette
Fingering Weight
100% Peruvian Highland Wool

Gloss Lace
Lace Weight
70% Wool, 30% Silk

Alpaca Cloud
Lace Weight
100% Baby Alpaca

Luminance
Lace Weight
100% Silk

Aloft
Lace Weight
72% Super Kid Mohair, 28% Silk

Shadow
Lace Weight
100% Merino Wool

View these beautiful yarns and
more at www.KnitPicks.com